How
To
Manage
Money

COVER DESIGN: FLORENCE ANDERSON
COPYRIGHT 1983 BY SPIROS ZODHIATES
PRINTED IN THE UNITED STATES OF AMERICA
ALL RIGHTS RESERVED
ISBN 0-89957-561-7
LIBRARY OF CONGRESS 82-74455

Canadian orders
Purpose Products
34 Berczy Street
Aurora, Ont. L4G 1W9

AMG Publishers, Chattanooga, TN 37422

First Printing, February 1983
Second Printing, January 1984

DEDICATION

Dedicated to my beloved son-in-law and daughter,
Paul and Lois Jenks,
who have practiced what the parable in Luke 16:1-9
teaches, having gone to the foreign mission field
to serve the Lord Jesus Christ and obtain
a welcoming committee in heaven.

How To Manage Money

by Spiros Zodhiates, Th.D.

**An exegetical exposition of
the Parable of the "Unjust" Steward
from the Greek Text (Luke 16:1-13)**

AMG PUBLISHERS

PREFACE

There is no more puzzling parable given by our Lord than that recorded in Luke 16:1-9. Many people stop with verse 9. However, it is absolutely necessary for the consequent teaching of our Lord to be examined for the full significance of the parable to be understood. I have searched far and wide in my 40,000 book library to find an adequate explanation of this parable erroneously called "The Parable of the Unjust Steward," but I could not. No interpretation could satisfy my inquisitive mind and hungry heart. Therefore, I gave myself to the meticulous examination and analysis of every word. I spared no time and effort. Finally I came up with what I believe is a cohesive and acceptable interpretation. Study it carefully and you will derive great lessons from it.

These studies were given in segments of seven minute devotionals to our staff at AMG International in Chattanooga and then typed. My editorial assistant of many years, Mrs. Dorothy Bryant, put it all together so it could appear in written form.

Then I discovered that I missed the examination of verse 13. This treatise I wrote down; hence the perceptible difference in style.

My thanks to my wife, Joan, who worked hard on this difficult manuscript making many valuable suggestions and improvements.

This study may change your whole attitude toward material things. You will be ahead in the long run if it helps you so to manage your money, which is but a trust, so it can assure for you a wonderful welcoming committee in heaven. It will make heaven so precious and life on earth so much more pleasurable. That is my prayer for you as you study this wonderful parable.

Spiros Zodhiates

Chattanooga, TN
October 21, 1982

CONTENTS

1

A Look at Luke 16:1-13
From a Different Viewpoint

In Luke 16:1-13 we have a parable concerning a rich man and his steward or business manager. It is admittedly one of the most difficult parables to interpret. First of all, let me translate it from the Greek text and then try to explain it as we go along to find out what the Lord is teaching us.

"And he was saying to his disciples, There was a rich man (He is not condemning rich people or riches here) who had an economist." That's the exact meaning of the Greek word, which can be interpreted as "business manager." Nowadays a person goes to a university to study economics, the science of managing money so it can be productive for its owner. "And this one [the economist] was accused," but the Greek word for accused is *diebleethee,* which is related to the word for devil. In Greek the devil is known as *diabolos.* But the verb to act like a devil is *diaballoo.* What does it mean? *Dia* means "through" and *balloo* is "to throw." It is "to go in between" or to separate, and that is the work of the devil. He is a slanderer. He goes in between, as for instance between a husband and a wife or a church and its pastor, and tries to separate them.

Here he comes between an employer and an employee.

The Steward Falsely Accused

Now the verb *diaballoo* cannot mean anything good, and therefore it cannot refer to correct accusations. Since this verb comes from the word that is the name for the devil, it has to signify a false accusation. As the greatest Greek lexicographers, Liddell and Scott, state, it is "to set at variance, make a quarrel between, to slander, to calumniate, to deceive by false accounts." This rich man, then, accepted a false or devilish accusation against his business manager. Unless you understand this correctly you cannot understand the parable.

The literal Greek of verse 1 is, "And this one was falsely accused unto him," to his boss, the rich man. Somebody came and said, "Hey, have you heard what your business manager is doing?" And he falsely accused him "as wasting his belongings."

And how the rich man responded to this false accusation is found in verse 2: "And having called him, he said unto him, What is this that I hear about you? Give an accounting of your economy, for you cannot be an economist anymore." I wonder if he investigated the accusation. It doesn't seem so. He evidently just took it for granted that the accusation was correct.

You know, the people who put the title on this parable were not inspired! They called this "The Parable of the Unjust Steward," but they ought to have called it "The Parable of the Unjust Employer"! He fired his business manager on sheer hearsay. Instead of investigating and looking into the books to see whether this accusation was true or not, he let him go.

How to React to Accusations Against Another Person

Now, every accusation has a chance of being either right

or wrong, and it ought to be carefully considered before pronouncing judgment. If it is right, the boss has the opportunity to do one of two things: either fire the person—and he is justified in doing so—or in asking him, "What do you intend to do? Are you sorry for what you did, or not? And if I give you another chance will you prove worthy of my trust?" I have been told that some of the best administrators of the greatest companies in America are people who started their business life by embezzling. But they repented and became the most faithful of business managers. "Repent and prove yourself honest and capable." It was up to the boss to offer this option. Forgiveness and giving a person a second chance sometimes pays dividends, but this rich man was not magnanimous.

In verse 2 we read, "And having called him, he said unto him, What is this I hear about you? Give an accounting of your economy." That is fine, but he didn't wait for it. And this is apparent from his next words, "For you cannot be an economist anymore." His decision was immediate. He believed the accusation without waiting for proof.

The business manager had no recourse. He had to take it. But apparently the actual severance was not immediate. Naturally, a business manager has a lot of things outstanding that he has to set in order. His employer may have said, "You have four weeks to get everything in order, and then you are through."

Now in verse 3 we find the business manager departing from the rich man's office and speaking to himself. "And the economist said unto himself, [sometimes it is good to talk to yourself when you're trying to think things out] What am I going to do?" This is in the future tense, *ti poieesoo*. He was looking to the future, to the one month hence when he would no longer be there. "What am I going to do so that when I am removed from my job . . ."

13

Metastasize: A Greek Word With a Double Meaning

Now when you read your English translation you find it extremely difficult to understand this pattern, because you don't know what the word for "removed" is in the original Greek. It is *metastathoo*, "when I am *metastasized* from my job." This is a very peculiar word. Any doctor, any nurse knows its meaning, for it is one of those Greek words that is constantly used in medical terminology. A patient goes to a doctor and says, "I have a lump here."

"Um," he says, after certain tests, "that's cancer."

And then about two or three months later the patient goes to the doctor again and says, "Doctor, I have a lump over here," and the doctor will use the term, "Your cancer has metastasized." What does he mean? It has moved on to another place. It has spread. The verb *methisteemi* or *methistanoo* is made up of the preposition *meta,* after or elsewhere, and the verb *histeemi,* to cause to stand. It is used also in Acts 13:22 in relation to the removing of King Saul through his rejection by God and later by bringing about his death (W. E. Vine). From this verb is derived the noun *metastasis. Meta* means "after" and *stasis* means "stand." Metastasize means "to stand after."

The phrase "he has passed on to the eternal habitations" as in verse 9 was very common in Greek (*Metestee eis tas aioonious monas* or *skeenas*). In the large Lexicon of the Greek Language by D. Demetrakou as the ninth meaning of the verb *methisteemi* is given as "to die" involving one's removal from life (Vol. 5, p. 4523). In Vol. 6, pp. 4629 and 4230 the fourth meaning of the noun *metastasis* is given as "the departure from life, death." The same meaning both to the verb and noun is attributed also by lexicographers Liddell and Scott (pp. 930-931 and 952).

Very interestingly, the Greeks today still use the word

metastasis and the verb *methisteemi* to indicate the removal of a person from this world to the next. If I were to refer to my brother as my metastasized brother, any Greek would know immediately that I was speaking about my dead brother. He has been metastasized; he has gone from this world to the next. Now, in this parable the Lord is trying to teach us about a man who is being removed or metastasized from his job. And the application to be made to ourselves here is that all of us are going to be metastasized from the world in which we now live. What do we do from the moment we realize this?

Preparing for Our Future

That the Lord is drawing a parallel in this parable between the removal of the steward from his position as a business manager and our removal or metastasis from this life, there can be no doubt. He speaks of the friends whom we should make during our life of faith as stewards of God's grace and forgiveness and who will welcome us "in the eternal habitations." Doesn't that involve our removal or metastasis from this world?

We have said that this parable is commonly known as that of the Unjust Steward, but that is a misnomer; he was the Wise Steward, as we shall see him called by our Lord in verse 8. Now the basic reason for which our Lord gave us this parable is to show us how this steward used his time from the moment that he knew he was going to lose his job. And in using the word metastasized, the Lord equates the removal from his position with removal from this world. Incidentally, the verb *metastathoo* being in the first aorist subjunctive passive tense indicates a specific future time at which the economist was going to be removed from his job, even as we are going to be removed from this world. It is in the passive voice which means that someone else was going to remove

15

him from his position. It was not going to be a voluntary resignation. Our departure from this world for the eternal habitations similarly is not going to be voluntary but on orders from our Lord. There is a definite time of our stewardship of God's grace upon this earth. The reason why the Lord did not prescribe a definite time that the steward was going to cease his service from the time of the announcement about his being fired is to indicate our ignorance of the exact time of our forthcoming *metastasis*. When we are going to be metastasized from this earth and thus end our opportunity of making friends who will welcome us in the eternal habitations no one knows. This was meant to cause us to maximize the use of every opportunity as it comes to us.

The steward realized he was going to face a very difficult situation when his firing became effective. But he also realized that there should be something he could do while still the business manager under fire. This we gather from verse 3: "And the economist said unto himself, What am I going to do now that my lord is taking away my economy, or my business, or my work from me?" Observe that he knew his limitations: "To dig, I am unable." He was a white-collar worker, but he realized that the only job that he could readily get would be common manual labor. And he says, "I cannot go out and work as a common laborer; to beg I am ashamed." This indicates that the man would be in extreme need the moment he was out of work. Obviously he did not have any money stashed away—another reason for believing he must have served his rich master honestly. It doesn't take long for somebody dealing with a great deal of money to yield to the temptation to feather his own nest. Then, if he is dismissed, he can say, "Well, I don't have to worry; I have a lot of your money. Go ahead and fire me. I can take care of myself."

But this was not the case with this man. "I cannot go out

and get just any job because, after all, I am in a managerial position. Those jobs that suit me are not easily available. And I cannot go and beg." But the plight of his impending joblessness spurred him on to do something immediately. Now, while he was still business manager, he decided to use the little time that he had available before he actually left his job to provide for his future. "I know what I am going to do so that, when I am metastasized, when I am removed, I may have a secure future."

Remember that through our Lord's use of this word *metastasis*, He was referring to the life after this one. The moment that you become a Christian you must begin to realize that this life is not forever, that your *metastasis* will come. This life is going to be terminated, even as the steward's job was going to be terminated whether he liked it or not. Note the parallel situation here. The boss came and said to him, "Man, you are fired!" Could the steward do anything about it? Absolutely nothing. The boss was sovereign. Of course, in our employee-employer relationships, what we say shouldn't be absolute. But remember that in a parabolic situation the reality cannot be symbolized perfectly by illustrative comparisons. The Lord is sovereign. Nevertheless, there is a parallelism here: the Lord is the One who speaks the last word in the life of each and every one of us. There comes a day when He says, "It's time for you to go," time for your *metastasis*, and there isn't anything that your doctor or your money or your education can do to prevent it. When God says it's time to leave this world, you go. Then it is too late to begin to do the things that count, the things you want to be remembered for, either on this earth or in eternity. Too late. The time to begin to do the things that are important in your life is the very moment you become a believer in Jesus Christ. Your first thought should be, "This life on earth is not forever;

17

therefore the things that count for eternity will have priority in my life." Don't be like someone who greatly distinguished himself in worldly achievements. In his last moments, he exclaimed, "I have provided in the course of my life for everything except death; and now, alas! I am to die, although entirely unprepared." How or when one dies is not important. The important thing is to prepare for the unavoidable happening while you are alive.

Now what was the thing that was most important for this steward? How to make friends who would take him into their homes when his job was terminated.

Life is so short, so uncertain. It is here one moment and gone the next—not because we want it that way, but because a sovereign God stops our heart from beating, and all is over as we await our eternal reward or punishment. May God give us the consciousness of the limitation of life, and bring the reality of *metastasis* to each one of us, that we will be going from this world to the next, and we had better begin doing what is important right now.

THINK IT OVER

1. In reading your King James Version, did you ever stop to wonder why the Lord would "commend" an "unjust steward" (see Luke 16:8)?
2. This parable is an excellent example of why we should look more deeply into seeming contradictions in the Bible by going back to the original language whenever possible.
3. What is the basic message of this parable?

2

A Wise Decision

As we continue studying the parable of the unjustly accused steward, we find him asking himself what he was going to do to assure his future in the short time before his ultimate dismissal. He decided the best thing to do was to use this time to make friends who would be of great help to him afterwards.

Similarly our Lord wants to teach us through this parable what should be our greatest concern from the moment that we become believers till the time of our removal from this world, our *metastasis*. Also we should learn that there is a relationship between how we are going to fare after our removal from this world and what we do in the interval between our conversion and death.

Will Every Believer Enjoy Heaven Equally?

God's eternal law of sowing and reaping applies to that as well. A farmer can expect a great crop if he sows the right seed, waters it and attends to its proper cultivation. Unfortunately, some people think that because they have accepted the Lord Jesus Christ as their Savior, it doesn't matter how they live, whether sacrifically or selfishly. They think every believer is going to enjoy heaven equally. I believe that this doctrine is a cause of much lukewarmness in the Church, allowing Christians to live in a way that is not worthy of the name of Jesus Christ.

Our Lord is teaching us here, and throughout the New Testament, that heaven is not going to be equally rewarding for everyone. There is a basic joy of heaven that comes as a result of our acceptance of the Lord Jesus Christ as our personal Savior. That is the acceptance of undeserved grace, but from that moment on there should be a yearning for deserved grace. Isn't that what the fifth beatitude of our Lord in Matthew 5:7 means? "Blessed the merciful for they shall obtain mercy." When? In heaven. (See author's study on the Beatitudes: *The Pursuit of Happiness* pp. 355 to 414. AMG Publishers.)

Have you ever noticed what James 2:12 and 13 says? Let me exegetically paraphrase it for you from the Greek: "Thus speak and thus do (life consists of words and works) as if you are going to be judged by a law of liberality. For the judgment (of the believer in regard to his works) will be without mercy to him (the believer) who did no mercy or who was not merciful. Mercy or mercifulness boasts against judgment." In other words, your mercifulness on earth will obtain mercy for you from God for your failures in life. This speaks of the counterbalancing of your earthly shortcomings through your mercifulness. (See author's volume on the book of James, Vol. I, *The Work of Faith*, AMG Publishers.)

Our joy of heaven will be proportionate to our rewards in heaven. Each of us is going to be a needy person at the end of the road, just as this business manager realized he was going to be, and that need is going to be met only as we engage in influencing people to be our friends by winning them to Christ—not through the accumulation of money for ourselves.

Winning Friends: The Steward's First Priority and Ours

This steward could have used the short interim he had left before the actual time of his dismissal to say, "All right, now I am going to steal from my master. He has a lot of money. Why should he have so much and I so little? I work hard; I deserve it. I am going to get all I can in the little time I have left."

No, he realized this was not going to serve him after his *metastasis*. He had a better idea. "How can I influence people?" he asked himself. "How can I make friends now, using my present influence while still a business manager, in order that these friends may prove to be of help to me when I am dismissed from my job?"

And it's true that everybody we make a friend by winning him or her to Jesus Christ is going to be a star in our crown for eternity. It is better to influence people for Christ while we can, in our work and walk of faith, than to do anything else while God spares us in life.

Remember that one of Satan's greatest tools is to persuade us that we must preoccupy ourselves with our problems instead of showing concern for others. The time to show mercifulness is when you are in dire need of it yourself. Dwight Moody used to speak of a tight farmer recently converted to whom a neighbor in distress appealed for help. The miser decided to prove the genuineness of his conversion by giving him a ham. On his way to get it the tempter whispered, "Give him the smallest one you have." A struggle ensued and finally the miser took down the largest ham he had. "You are a fool," the devil said. And the farmer replied,

21

"If you don't keep still, I'll give him every ham in the smokehouse!"

We realize that our *metastasis* is coming. How tragic if we must face it without knowing that we have made friends for Christ by being the stewards of His grace on this earth. May God give us a consciousness of the priorities that should govern our life as believers.

As we study this parable, we cannot know whether our Lord was basing it on an actual case history, or not. But such things do happen, and it is so true to life, that I am going to look at it as something that actually took place and do a character study in depth of the two principal characters involved.

Apparently this business manager was so dedicated to his employer's interests that he didn't have time to socialize and make friends. You know, this is characteristic of many dedicated people—pastors, missionaries, and heads of religious and charitable organizations. They are busy night and day, hardly having time for social life, and in consequence they don't get to know people intimately, to make real friends. When trouble comes to them, they have no one to turn to.

How the Steward Solved His Problem of Making Friends

Now, let us look at the way this steward figured out how to handle his situation. He said, "I am still the business manager for a little while until I am finally dismissed. How can I use this position to my advantage in order to gain friends?" We read about his solution in verses 5 and 6: "And having invited one of the debtors of his lord, he said unto the first, How much do you owe my lord? And he said, one hundred measures of oil." In those days they measured what they owed in merchandise.

22

"And he said unto him, Receive this document, and having sat down write fifty." In other words, "I, as the business manager, have the right to forgive any debt that is due my lord. And I forgive you fifty percent of your indebtedness." Some people may say this was a dishonest act. But it really was not. It was in his power as business manager to set terms for the payment of past-due accounts. It would have been dishonest if he had said to himself, "Well, I am going to forgive this man fifty percent, but my hand is under the table, and part of that will come to me personally." He didn't do anything of the sort. He acted within his power.

For instance, in my business transactions, I, as the President of AMG International, may decide to forgive a debt due to the Mission for some valid reason. It is not a dishonest act. It is my prerogative because of my position. Maybe a person is so valuable to the Mission that I feel led to forgive his indebtedness on that account. The reason this steward forgave this indebtedness was so that this person might be indebted to him as a friend. Always remember one thing, however—that symbolism does not represent the reality of a parable. It cannot be pressed too far. The physical illustration can never fully explain spiritual truth. For instance, can there be a physical material illustration of the Trinity, that God is in three persons, the Father, the Son and the Holy Spirit? Impossible. Spiritual truths can only be imperfectly and inadequately illustrated by physical realities known to us. The important thing in a parable is to conceive its basic lesson. The parts cannot fit perfectly together for they are physical parts illustrating a spiritual whole.

And he called the second man (in verse 7) and said, "How much do you owe? And he said one hundred bushels of wheat. And he said unto him, Receive this document and write eighty." "I forgive you twenty percent."

Now I want you to note that sin is presented as a debt. In teaching us to pray, "And forgive us our debts as we forgive our debtors" (Matthew 6:12), our Lord was referring to sin. In Luke 13:4 our Lord in speaking of those who died when the tower of Siloam collapsed, said, "Think ye that they were sinners above all men that dwelt in Jerusalem?" The word for sinners here in Greek is *opheiletai* meaning debtors. We, as the stewards of the grace of God, have the great privilege of declaring the forgiveness that there is in Jesus Christ to others. That is equivalent to the writing off of their debts. Somebody confesses his sin and says, "I am indeed a debtor to the Lord, I am a sinner." And the Lord authorizes us as His representatives to declare to this repentant person, "Because Jesus Christ died for you, your sins are remitted. You are forgiven." Not because of what we have done, but because of what Jesus has done, and the authority He has given in John 20:23: "Whose soever sins ye remit, they are remitted unto them; and whose soever sins ye retain, they are retained." And so we declare Christ's forgiveness to people, just as this steward forgave the debtors of his lord. This is the greatest message any of us can proclaim: the forgiveness that is to be found in the Lord Jesus Christ.

> Tell men about the Master,
> Of the wrong He freely forgave,
> Of His love and tender compassion,
> Of His love that is mighty to save;
> For men's hearts are aweary, aweary
> Of the woes and temptations of life,
> Of the error that stalks in the noonday,
> Of falsehood and malice and strife.
> —Author Unknown

The controller of any organization knows that each month there are certain debts that are written off because

24

they cannot be collected. I know that in the statements I receive each month from our controller, he never asks me as the President of the organization whether certain bad debts should be written off; he just goes ahead and does it. That is part of his work. That is part of any business manager's work.

And you know, things haven't changed. There were people in Jesus' day who didn't pay their debts, and there are people today who don't pay them. Now this steward knew who the bad debtors were, and he used his brains. The Lord wants us to use our brains, too. Why not officially forgive bad debts and make the debtor your friend! In fact, a little later on in this parable, He tells us that the people of the world are sometimes smarter in such matters than the people of God. This is not a very good commentary on our stewardship or business sense. Anyhow, this man called two of the debtors of his Lord, and reduced their indebtedness by fifty percent and twenty percent respectively, for cash on the line. Getting some money is better than none. That's smart business.

Many people have misunderstood this action on his part, calling it a dishonest act; but not if you allow a little leeway for his ingenuity in collecting part of the bad debts at all. And not if you see that he did not ask for a personal kickback for doing this favor. It was just inherent in his action that these people would appreciate it, just as if I were to write a letter to a debtor of AMG and say, "I realize your difficulties; I realize that you cannot pay the full amount; so this debt can be written off in part."

Not Every Detail of a Parable Can Be Pressed for Its Literal Meaning

As I said at the beginning, no parable that our Lord gave corresponds fully in all its details to the reality that He was trying to teach. Each parable has a basic meaning, and only in its basic meaning must we take it literally, and not necessarily in all its details. The basic meaning here is that just as this business manager acted from the time that he knew he was going to depart from his job, so must we act from the time that we become believers until our *metastasis* comes, our departure from this world. This man wanted to make friends during that period of time. Our Lord indicates that the greatest thing we can do in the world as believers is to make friends by leading others to our Friend and Savior, Jesus Christ.

THINK IT OVER

1. What are the basic priorities in your life?
   a. Providing bountifully for yourself and your loved ones?
   b. Building a fat bank account?
   c. Seeking recognition and honor from your associates by making a name for yourself?
   d. Or? _____

   _____

2. In studying a parable, should you take every detail literally, or look for the basic lesson?

3

How to Live
in View of the
Certainty of Death

Often in the Scriptures we, the believers, are called stewards. We are given the privilege of proclaiming God's forgiveness and grace. Paul in I Corinthians 4:1 calls us the "stewards of the mysteries of God." Certainly the declaration of the forgiveness of an undeserving sinner is nothing short of a mystery. Why let him go free? Because Jesus Christ paid the price. And, indeed, as the rich employer bore the burden of the forgiven debts of these bad debtors, so Jesus Christ bears the price and burden of the repentant people to whom we proclaim His forgiveness. Paul says of a bishop in Titus 1:7, "For a bishop must be blameless, as the steward of God . . . ." And Peter delineating Christian conduct in the light of the times in which we live says: "As every man hath received the gift (charisma), even so minister the same one to another as good stewards of the manifold grace of God." The principal task of every charismatic (the recipient of God's grace) is to declare God's grace as a good steward of it. We proclaim to others that there is forgiveness of the debt of sin in Jesus

Christ. How wonderful to be able to say, "Do you realize that your indebtedness to God can be written off if you simply repent and believe that there is forgiveness with the One to whom you are a debtor?"

Now our Lord actually told His disciples that they could say this with authority, in John 20:23: "If of some you remit their sins . . . ." Can you or I forgive sin, can we remit sins? Only in the same manner as the steward remitted the indebtedness of the debtors to his lord. It was not an inherent right of his own. He was acting only as a steward, as a declarer of the forgiveness of his lord. When Jesus said to His disciples, "If of some you remit their sins," He was saying that these sins are forgiven by the Lord to whom the debt is due. That is what you and I can do—declare the grace of God. Scripture tells us that men's sins have already been forgiven. You and I simply declare the forgiveness.

"And if of some you retain, they have been retained." That refers to the unrepentant, who feel no need of or desire for God's forgiveness when we proclaim it to them. But if they repent, if they accept this forgiveness as the debtors in the parable had to do, they will fulfill their part of the contract offered them.

Forgiveness Conditional on Acceptance

Do you remember what the steward said in Luke 16:6 and 7? "Take this document and write quickly that you are forgiven fifty percent, that you are forgiven twenty percent." And if a person who was a debtor did not write his name indicating an acceptance of this forgiveness, his debt could not be forgiven.

Even so, we can declare that there is forgiveness in Jesus Christ, and he who accepts our offer of forgiveness—not because we have earned the right to grant it, but in our capacity as stewards of our Lord—is forgiven by God. If that person to whom we declare forgiveness extends his hand in acceptance, we can say to him, "Your sins are forgiven; your debt is wiped out."

Of course, we may wonder, why the steward offered only fifty percent and twenty percent of forgiveness. I have no answer to that. It may be, and it's only conjecture, that partial forgiveness is spoken of here because we know that there is a duty from every debtor of God in the future to fulfill his responsibility toward God. God forgives our sins, but this doesn't absolve us of our own responsibility of living for Him, working for Him, and seeking by His grace to "Go and sin no more."

In Luke 16:8 we read, "And the Lord commended the unjust steward . . . ." On the surface of it, it looks as if the Lord were condoning evil. But actually the translation should be, "And the Lord commended the economist [or the steward] of unrighteousness . . . ."

Why Did the Lord Equate Money With Unrighteousness?

What are we to understand by the word "unrighteousness" here? Look carefully at another Scripture which uses the same expression. Acts 1:18 speaks of Judas who received thirty pieces of silver. He took money in order to betray the Lord Jesus Christ. Let me translate this directly from the Greek New Testament: "He therefore acquired a field with the reward of unrighteousness," or "by means of unrighteousness." The word which the Authorized Version translated as "iniquity" is *adikia*, unrighteousness, as in Luke 16:8. What is that unrighteousness? It is money. The Lord spoke of money as unrighteousness. Why? Well, it is not only today that thieves break into a place to steal in order to get money to use for evil purposes, such as drugs. That is an unrighteous

29

use of money. And our Lord chose to call money unrighteousness in this parable to demonstrate that, as the world
uses money for unrighteous purposes, we as believers, in
contrast to that, must use our money for righteous purposes.

"The steward of unrighteousness," therefore, was a steward
of money. He dealt with his lord's money. And we deal with
our Lord's money too, for the money that you and I have is
not ours, it is the Lord's. Dare we ever use it for unrighteous
purposes? This steward used money in a proper manner and
the Lord commended him for it. He used money to make
friends. That was the wisest use of money. It was money that
belonged to his lord, although he had worked hard for it. In
our case as believers we must consider money in our hands as
really the Lord's although we have worked to earn it.

Notice also that exactly the same expression is used a little
farther on when Jesus speaks of the "mammon of unrighteousness" in Luke 16:9: "by means of the mammon of
unrighteousness." Here we have exactly the same phrase.
They don't translate it in the same manner as in verse 8,
"unjust," in the phrase "the unjust steward," but here they
correctly translate it as "the mammon of unrighteousness,"
not "the unrighteous mammon." That is one of the reasons
why I believe the correct translation of verse 8 is "the steward
of unrighteousness," meaning "money." And what is the
mammon of unrighteousness? Mammon means the god of
money, the god of unrighteousness.

In this connection, there is one more expression where
this word is used, this time as an adjective. It occurs in verse
11, which says, "If, therefore, you have not been faithful in
the unrighteous mammon." What it means is that mammon,
the god of money, is indeed unjust, is indeed unrighteous.

So we have three expressions. The first is "the economist
of unrighteousness" in verse 8, meaning the economist of

money; and the second expression, in verse 9, is "the mammon of unrighteousness," the god of money; and the third expression, in verse 11, is "the unjust mammon," the mammon that is unjust in his actions. So the translation of verse 8 is now clear: "And the lord commended the steward of unrighteousness [or of money]."

Our Heavenly Father is a righteous God. The Lord Jesus Christ never commends anybody who does anything unrighteous or unjust; but He looks upon us to see how we use money, that which may be used for righteous or unrighteous purposes. May God give us the wisdom to know how to use His gift of money as good and faithful stewards.

The interest of this business manager was to make as many friends as possible, for he knew that one day soon he would need them. The loneliest person is one who doesn't make friends. We should never be so conceited as to think we will ever be free of the need of friends in this life.

This man proceeded to use his position as business manager to forgive some bad debts people owed his lord. It was not dishonest, because the Lord said it was not. We read in verse 8, "And the Lord commended the economist of unrighteousness," as I have already explained. And then our Lord added that he acted wisely. Now how on earth—and this is the quarrel I have with the translators—could our Lord commend an unrighteous steward and then say that he did wisely? Impossible! He commended him because he acted wisely.

In what did the wisdom of his action consist? First, this man looked at the time that he had available before his dismissal from his job became effective and he said, "I only have a limited time to do what is necessary to secure that which I may need when I am out of work." He was going to be dismissed and he knew he was going to need assistance, hospitality from the friends that he would have to make.

Why God Does Not Tell Us How Long We Shall Live on Earth

We are not told how much time this man was given before his final dismissal as business manager. And God does not say to a believer, when he first receives Christ, "I sign a contract with you promising that you will live twenty years, five months, three hours and four seconds," or anything like it. He doesn't reveal the time of our departure from this world.

Would you have liked Him to? We must allow God to have a little more wisdom than that. There could be no greater mistake in anybody's life than to know the time of his departure from this world. Do you know why? Because the Lord wants us to live all the time as if today would be our last. I believe it was John Wesley who was asked at one time, "What would you do if you knew that tonight you would die?" And that great preacher of years gone by said, "I would do exactly what I have scheduled to do." Could you say that? Could I say that? That if I knew that my time, my *metastasis,* would come at a certain date, I wouldn't change my plans at all? The uncertainty of our *metastasis* from this world is not a curse but a blessing, for it creates in us a desire to do our best every moment. If we knew we had another year, another month, we might say, "Well, I can be slack because I still have time." But the Lord wants each of us to live as if we would not have another chance, and therefore we are motivated to attach ourselves completely to the priorities not only of this life but also of eternity. He is wise who lives as if today were his last day, as if this hour were his last hour, as if his contribution to God's work, and the exercise of his talent, gave him a last opportunity of doing something that would count for eternity.

This, perhaps, was the wisdom exercised by the lord of

this steward in not fixing an exact date. He probably said, "When you are finished with your work, then you can leave." And God says, "When you are all finished, then I will call you home." It may be that God cuts short your life and mine, if we are believers, when He feels that we are not going to contribute anything more to His Kingdom. And He may cut the life of the unbeliever short when He feels that giving him another chance to live would only add to his punishment in eternity. Such a decision is always brought about by the benevolence of God. God is most wise in regulating the time alloted to us from the moment we believe until the time of our *metastasis*. May we take advantage of the opportunities for service in Christ's Kingdom as if this were our last day on earth.

THINK IT OVER

1. Have you ever assured anyone that his sins are forgiven if he will repent and receive Christ?
2. When you receive your paycheck, or draw money from the bank, whose money do you consider it?
   a. Your own to do with as you please?
   b. The Lord's to be apportioned as He would have you?
3. Would you like to know how long you are going to live? How would you feel if you *did* know? Is God kind in withholding this information from us?
4. Why is this uncertainty good for us in the long run?

4

Using Our
Time, Talents
and Money for Christ

After saying that this business manager had acted wisely, our Lord says that the sons of this generation are wiser than the sons of light in their own generation. What did He mean? It was a polite rebuke to those who are the sons of light, whose main task it is to propagate the light. The sons of light are not doing as good a job in winning people to their side as the people of darkness are doing in winning people to theirs.

Let me give you an example: Cable TV is a good illustration. It is supposed to be the most dangerous pornographic medium in America. The world, the powers of darkness, are taking it over and using it to the greatest advantage in the propagation of darkness, of sin.

The Gospel Hindered by Lack of Business Acumen

What do we, the sons of light, do? We expect the people to come to church to be exposed to the Gospel, and we put up a building that costs three million dollars and is used three or four hours a week. "There is something wrong," the Lord says, "with you Christians. You don't know how to do it. You lack business acumen." And if you examine the parables of our Lord you will find that He is constantly striking a pact. "I give you one pound; I am pleased with the one who produces ten, not the one who says, All that God expects of me is to be found faithful." No, He also expects us to be fruitful.

Suppose a business man manufactures something that can make housework easier. However, no woman will come to his store to buy that piece of equipment unless she knows the product is there and what it can do for her. A wise business man doesn't simply manufacture and store a whole warehouse of merchandise. He sends out the word; he blasts television, radio and the newspapers to tell the world out there what he has down here.

What do we Christians do? Put four walls around us, and nobody knows what is going on inside unless we go to them.

Use Public Media to Spread the Gospel Outside the Walls of the Church

I believe this is an excellent parable to illustrate the wisdom of using the public media of communications in getting the Gospel out. Take newspaper evangelism, for instance. When I was a 16-year-old living in Cairo, Egypt, I had a great burden to reach every Greek family in Cairo. There were about 100,000 of them, and they all read a newspaper that was published in the Greek language. Every Greek family received this newspaper. There I was with a desire to communicate the message of the Gospel to all my fellow Greeks. What did I do? Sit down and say, "Lord reveal the need of the Gospel to every Greek in Cairo? Send them to me so that I can give them the Gospel. Lord, take the fish out of the sea and put them in my tub!" No, I had the wisdom to see that if I was going to reach everybody in Cairo I must do everything I could to put the Gospel in the medium which reached these people. And this is where the idea of newspaper evangelism was born.

Oh, I knew realism must be the twin sister of idealism. That was the idea, but immediately I asked, "How is it possible to do this?" I felt that the Greeks were so fanatical that they would never allow an evangelical Christian ever to publish a Gospel message in their newspapers. I knew all that, but at the same time, if I know the best way of doing something, I will never choose a lesser way to accomplish the most.

It took many years. I remember the first time I walked into the office of a Greek newspaper in Cairo, they wouldn't even let me past the first secretary or the receptionist. A few years later, when the Lord opened almost all the newspapers and magazines of Greece, they couldn't help it. They said, "He is all over the place. And if we don't carry his articles, our paper will be considered lacking." And to this very day the Gospel published as a paid advertisement in this newspaper reaches every Greek in Cairo, Egypt, and I live in the United States.

Your Money Belongs to God; Use It Wisely for Him

The Lord is saying, "The world is wise; they know how to use their money to accomplish the most. Get the message, My disciples; get the message, Christians; be effective in how you spend your money, for it isn't yours, it is God's money." And that is the message that we must hear and apply.

May God help us to be as wise as the world in the investment of our time, of our talents, and of our money to accomplish the most with the least, in the way that pleases Him the greatest.

In Luke 16:9 the Lord gives us a commandment: "And I say unto you, Make to yourselves friends (by means) of the mammon of unrighteousness; that, when ye fail, [in other words, when you die], they may receive you to everlasting habitations." If you have a more modern translation than the King James Version, it is quite possible that this verse reads differently. Instead of "when ye fail" it may read "when it fails." The reason for this is that there are several texts or manuscripts from which translations have been made. The King James Version was made from the *Textus Receptus*, the "Received Text," which translates the Greek verb *eklipeete* as "when ye fail (die)." The Greek verb *ekleipoo* (first person singular) in this context means "to die." It is a compound verb made up of the preposition *ek* which means "from or out of" and the verb *leipoo* which means "to leave, quit, to die, to be killed, to be absent." The verb *ekleipoo* therefore means "to disappear from your present state of being, to quit your present circumstances and environment." It is exactly the word that is used in English to indicate the disappearance of the sun from our view, the eclipse of the sun. It is the obscuration of light from one celestial body by another. Actually what the Greek text says is: "When you are eclipsed" from this earth, when you disappear from here to go to the eternal habitations. (See Liddell and Scott: *A Greek-English Lexicon* and D. Demetrakou, *Lexicon of the Greek Language.*) This is a reference to our metastasis from earth, not the termination of money. The Lord says: When you are no more (*hotan eklipeete*), you the people, you and me, the Christians, when you depart from this world.

You recall that I said the key word to the understanding of this parable is *metastasis*, a word used by the Greeks to indicate the departure of man from this world to the next. And this is the basic lesson of this parable. As the steward was *metastasized*, or removed, from his job; so are we going to be *metastasized* or removed from this world. And when the

38

steward became aware of his imminent removal from his job, he immediately started to act so that what he did in the interim would secure his future. This was to make friends by forgiving part of their indebtedness to his lord, so that later on, when in need, these friends might take him into their homes.

This is the basic concept of the whole parable, and so when our Lord says, "Now when you are removed," He meant it was the steward who was going to be removed from his job, not the money removed from him, but he himself removed. Therefore, the second person plural of this verb, as the King James Version has it from the *Textus Receptus*, is in my opinion to be preferred exegetically, if we are to understand this parable.

A Welcoming Committee in Heaven

When we are removed, when we are no more on this earth but are in the eternal habitations, it is the people that we have won to Jesus Christ while we were on earth who are going to constitute our welcoming committee in heaven. Read the verse again and understand it: "And I say unto you, [our Lord now applies the parable] Make unto yourselves friends . . . ." That means that from the moment we become Christians, the most important task we can engage in is not to make money but to make friends and influence people for the Lord. "Make friends unto yourselves" does not mean that we should compromise our position and principles by being unequally yoked with unbelievers, either in marriage or as boon companions. This is not the meaning of it. The Greek word *philous*, "friends," refers to those who have the same interests as somebody else. Two teachers are friends because they have the common interest of teaching. Two hunters become friends because they have the common interest of hunting. To be friends with somebody is to have common interests with him or her. And when our Lord says to us as believers, "Make unto yourselves friends," He does not mean that we should be buddy-buddy with those who don't believe in God. "Can two walk together, except they be agreed?" (Amos 3:3). No, they cannot. The only way to enjoy a happy friendship is to have a friend who agrees with you in your basic beliefs.

So when our Lord says, "Make unto yourselves friends," He meant, "Use the money that has been delivered to you by God in order to preach the Gospel and win people to Jesus Christ; and these people will become your friends. They will have common interests with you, and when you get to heaven, your eternal habitations, they will be there to welcome you, and that will be the greatest joy that can happen to you."

As you look back upon your life, nothing will seem as important to you as the people you have won to Jesus Christ. Therefore, the best application that you can make of your money, of what many people use for unrighteousness, is to preach the Gospel and make friends for Christ. Your welcome in heaven will depend upon how many souls have been won in your life from the moment you believe until your *metastasis* comes. And the most important thing that you can do to get ready is to use the so-called filthy lucre to win souls to Christ, who will constitute your welcoming committee in heaven. I repeat, this is the basic lesson of this wonderful parable.

Another detail we must understand in this ninth verse is the preposition "of" in the phrase, "Make to yourselves friends *of* the mammon of unrighteousness." The Greek preposition *ek* could be better translated "by means of" or "with" as is translated in Matthew 27:7 and Acts 1:18. We should use our money to win people to Jesus Christ who, because of that, become our friends and who in turn will welcome us in the eternal habitations.

Why does the Lord call "money" the mammon of unrighteousness? In verse 8 He called money "unrighteousness." Now in verse 9 He calls it "mammon of unrighteousness." The word mammon (*mamoonas*) is used by our Lord in each instance that it occurs in the New Testament. In Matthew 6:24 He said, "Ye cannot serve God and mammon." It stands in the context of material things. Our Lord was implying that there is always the danger of making material things a false god in contrast to the true God who is Spirit in His essence and can meet both our spiritual and physical needs. The only other place where the word mammon occurs is in this parable, Luke 16:9, 11 and 13. As Cremer says, "It is the comprehensive word for all kinds of possessions, earnings, and gains, a designation of value" (*Biblico-Theological Lexicon of New Testament Greek*).

In Luke 6:9 it means "value of money." If we were to leave the word *adikias*, unrighteousness, to mean anything else than money, this verse would be very difficult to explain. Our Lord said to His disciples: "Make unto yourselves friends by means of the value of money, the very money that ungodly people use for unrighteous purposes. For you it has value in winning souls who will one day constitute your welcoming committee in heaven." Money in the hands of a disciple of Christ becomes a very valuable thing, not an end in itself as in the case of the unbeliever, but a means to a higher end. As the unbeliever makes possessions his god, his mammon, you should use them to lead people to the true God.

May our Heavenly Father teach us how to use our time, our talents, our money, before we close our eyes forever and cannot come back to do it over. May He grant each one of us a wonderful welcoming committee in heaven for having lived according to His will here on earth.

> When the voice of the Master is calling,
>   And the gates into Heaven unfold,
> And the saints of all ages are gathering
>   And are thronging the city of gold,
> How my heart shall o'erflow with rapture
>   If a brother shall greet me and say,
> "You pointed my footsteps to Heaven,
>   You told me of Jesus the Way."
>
> —Author Unknown

THINK IT OVER

1. What is your primary duty as a child of God:
   a. To be faithful in attending church?
   b. To propagate the Gospel? (Note: These are not mutually exclusive, but quite often the first does not include the second.)

2. How can you use your time, talents, and money most effectively for the Lord:
   a. By giving 10% to the church?
   b. By supporting the work of missions around the world?
   c. By volunteering your spare time to witnessing to others through tract distribution, mission work, etc.? (Again, these are not mutually exclusive uses of your time, talents, and money.)

3. What talents have you that Christ could use? Do you let Him?

5

Three Important Lessons

We have finished the main parable given by our Lord in the 16th chapter of Luke, in verses 1-9 primarily, about the rich man who dismissed his business manager on hearsay accusation. After giving this parable, the Lord added many down-to-earth lessons that we should take to heart.

Lesson Number One: All That God Gives Us Is a Sacred Trust in View of Eternity

I think the first lesson the Lord wants to teach us here is that in our everyday lives we must deal with everything that is entrusted to us, be it talent, money, or time, in view of its eternal value and consequence. This steward's foresight, as soon as he knew he was going to be dismissed from his job, led him to say, "What can I do now in order that, after my dismissal, I will have some friends who will be of assistance to me?" And with the same concern for the life to come, every time you feel like spending money you should say, "What can I do with this money in view of eternity?" Don't think of the luxuries it can buy, how much leisure it can afford you. Think of what it can do for eternity. Live every moment, every day so that it will count for eternity. Remember, there is no coming back to do it over. The first thing that every Christian must become aware of is that from the moment he is saved his life is changed. He deals with matter in a different way than the world does. He deals with it as an investment for eternity. Others can easily detect where lie our primary interests. Dwight L. Moody used to say that it does not take long to tell where a man's treasure is. In fifteen minutes' conversation with most men you can tell whether their treasures are on earth or in heaven.

Lesson Number Two: The Most Important Use of Money

The second lesson is on the most important use of money. This steward was an economist of money. And we learn here that our Lord approved of the fact that, from the moment he knew he was going to be the manager of his employer's wealth for only a little while longer, he did not try to acquire money for himself, but he endeavored to use his privileged position during that interval to make friends, to influence people. Our Lord wants to teach us that the most important use of money is not to gratify our pleasures, but to win others to Christ.

Every time you look at your wallet or your paycheck, I know that, humanly speaking, the temptation arises, "How can this improve my way of life? How much more can I buy with it? Can I buy a better home, perhaps, or use it to live a cut above the common standard?" It is part of our Adamic nature to want more pleasure, more comfort, more things. During World War II, posters everywhere queried the driver, "Is this trip necessary?" We are in a spiritual warfare, and we should analyze every purchase with the question, "Is this expenditure necessary?" Our Lord says, "Look at the material substances of life and say, 'How can this be used in order to influence people for Christ?' "

This lesson is basic to our everyday life. Take this parable with you to the supermarket. Take it with you to the clothing store. Take it with you to the shoe store. Take it with you to your desk while you are working. Ask, "How can my hours be used, not wasted, so that the most people may be influenced for Christ?" Take it with you when you wonder how you should spend a free hour or two. "Should I go somewhere I can find others who have never heard of Jesus Christ? Shall I let my light shine in a dark place, or shall I go only where everybody else is a Christian?" Fellowship with other Christians is not the paramount business of a Christian. What a Christian ought to seek is a place where his candle, small though it may be, can shine for Jesus Christ in some dark corner of the world. This is influencing people. You don't have to have a lot of money to influence others. All you have to have is the right philosophy of life, the attitude that says, "I am the light shining for Jesus Christ," and place yourself where there is so much darkness that no matter how little your light is, it can still show the way to others who don't have any light at all.
Can you say with the unknown poet:

God gave me something very sweet
 To be mine own this day:
A precious opportunity
 A word for Christ to say.

If so, you will have found one of the greatest joys life can hold.

Lesson Number Three: Make Friends in Order to Win Them to Christ

A third lesson is that we should make unto ourselves friends, win people to Jesus Christ, so that when we are no more, when our *metastasis* comes, when we die, they will welcome us in the eternal habitations. These are words that come out of the mouth of Jesus Christ. Would He have told us a lie when He said that beyond the grave there is conscious life?

God help us to learn these very important lessons: That we must live every moment and use everything that we possess in view of eternity; that we must consider people more important than money; and that we must know that death does not end all.

THINK IT OVER

1. Is your life compartmentalized: So much for me, so much for my family and others, so much for God?
2. Or does everything in your life come under the one umbrella: All for God, and the due proportion He lends me for basic needs to live as I should in view of eternal values?
3. Would living that way entail any changes in your life-style?
4. Review again the three basic lessons stressed in this chapter.

6

Should Christians Expect Immunity From Sickness and Death

The 16th chapter of Luke gives us more detailed information about life after death in the two parables it contains than almost any other portion of Scripture. The first is the Parable of the Unjust Capitalist, in verses 1-9; and the Parable, or story—call it whatever you wish, it makes no difference really—of the Rich Man and Lazarus. They both died and they both met with a situation that was real after death.

The first thing that I want to call to your attention in this 9th verse is our Lord's words, "When ye shall *eklipeete,*" meaning "you will be no more; out of sight." The King James translation is very unfortunate. It says, "When ye shall fail . . . ." But that is not the real meaning. The Lord was speaking here about our *metastasis*, our removal from this world to the next. The verb in Greek is *ekleipoo*, and it is the only place in the New Testament that it is used of death. It is used in other instances, as in Luke 22:32, where it refers to the missing or absence of faith, "that thy faith fail not," literally "when there shall be no faith." In Luke 23:45 it is used of the sun, "and the sun was darkened," literally "when the sun shall be no more" (shall disappear from view). It is used also of years in Hebrews 1:12, "and thy years shall not fail." When the faith, the sun, the years shall be no more is the meaning in each instance. They come to an end in their present being or state. But the only place it is used of human death is in Luke 16:9, "when you shall be no more . . . ." *Ekleipoo* means to be absent from your present state, "when you shall die."

False Teachings About Sickness and Death

In reading a book by a television personality whom millions of people listen to, I came across this statement: "If Jesus Christ came to take away sin and the consequences of sin which is death, He also came to take away sickness." Now, mind you, this steward whom the Lord commended died, but just think of what people today are teaching over the air and in their publications as in the above quoted book. "If a man can stand totally in the presence of Almighty God he will not be sick. He will not have illness in his life, nor can he have death because he is totally in the presence of God."

Our Lord's Teaching on the Subject

I submit to you that it is high time we paid attention to the teaching of Jesus Christ rather than the teaching of man. Our Lord says, "If ye, when ye shall be no more . . . ." That means "when you shall die," and you know perfectly well that death in your lifetime and mine is a reality. It is going to come, not necessarily because we are out of the will of God, but because Christ left yet unfinished the work for the redemption of our bodies. That redemption will come when we see the Lord face to face (Rom. 8:23).

Sickness and Death the Common Lot of All

Therefore do not be possessed with a sense of guilt when you have a headache, or when you lose a tooth, or when you develop ulcers. Just examine your life to see if you are not worrying too much, or abusing your body by neglecting to eat, sleep, and exercise as you know you should.

Death is part and parcel of the common crucible of humanity. It comes to believers and unbelievers alike. It is a dread event for unbelievers. It is a welcome calling home by the Lord for believers. Come early or late, whatever time it may come, it will be when God sees fit to take us. He may cut the cord of your life if you are a believer when He sees you have amassed the greatest glory for heaven. He may cut the cord of your life if you are an unbeliever when He sees that you are hopeless, that if you live longer you will amass more condemnation to yourself. He is wiser than you and I in terminating the life that He gives us only temporarily. We must realize that death is real; and what leads to death, sickness, is also real. May God help us to live in the full knowledge and assurance that we are going to give an accounting of our life to Him when this life is over.

Now, is sickness part of the lot of the believer, or am I outside of the will of God when I get sick? As a Christian, am I also out of the will of God when I die? Who is the liar—Jesus Christ or those people who tell you that as a Christian, when you are sick you are outside the will of God, and when you die you are outside the will of God?

Will We Know One Another in Heaven?

When Jesus told of the steward who died, He was speaking to His disciples, who should consider winning people to Jesus Christ far more important than making

49

money. He called death *metastasis,* a going from one place to another; that is what death is. What does He say will happen then? "They will welcome you." Who? The people that you have actually won to Jesus Christ by the proper use of your money. Will they know you in heaven? You have the word of Jesus Christ here that you will be a recognizable personality. When you die, you will not be a gaseous substance without form. You will have recognizable personality features. Will somebody know me? Yes, everybody will know me in heaven who knew me on earth, and I will know everybody else. Now, if they are going to welcome me into the eternal habitations, they have got to know who I am and what I have done for them. They have got to know that I have been responsible through my life on earth for leading them to Jesus Christ. They will receive me, they will recognize me, and I will recognize them.

And this one reason is why, for the Christian, death is so wonderful. We do not lose all our believing relatives when they die, but they become more alive than they have ever been before, because the limitations of time and space have been abolished.

"They will receive me." That is the second truth that you find here. They will receive you where? Well, the English text says, "Into everlasting habitations." The word "habitations" in the Greek text is *skeenas,* "tabernacles, tents." Why does our Lord say, "eternal tents"? What has eternity got to do with something that is so temporary as a tent? You remember that in John chapter 1 it speaks of Jesus Christ the eternal one, the *Logos,* the Word who had always been with the Father, and in the 14th verse we read, "And the Word became flesh, and dwelt among us." "Dwelt" is the King James translation of the verbal form of this word *skeenas,* "and tabernacled among us." Here the eternal Word who is Spirit, which is the essence of God, is also the essence of Jesus Christ. He came to live temporarily in human flesh. And here our Lord tells us that we are going to have "tents" in which we are going to dwell in heaven. What did He mean by that—"eternal tents"? This is just what the Apostle Paul meant when he spoke of "a spiritual body" in I Corinthians 15:44. (For a thorough exegesis of what is meant by spiritual body see the Author's 860-page exegesis of I Corinthians 15 entitled, "Conquering the Fear of Death," AMG Publishers, Chattanooga, TN 37421.)

THINK IT OVER

1. What is the basic mistake most people make in promoting the false teaching that sickness and death need not happen to a Christian?
   a. They take Scripture verses out of context.
   b. They ignore the teaching of Jesus Christ, and the experience of Paul, Timothy, Epaphroditus, and other devout believers in the Scripture.
2. Name three persons in the New Testament who appeared in visible, bodily form after their death to show that believers will recognize one another in heaven. (See Luke 9:29-31; 24:36-43.)

7

Eternal Life:
God's Gift to Believers Only

In Luke 16:9 we find much theology that we shall do well to consider. Jesus assured the steward in the parable, and He assures us, of course, by extension, that, if he made friends for Christ here, when he disappeared, when he was actually "eclipsed" (that is the word), then he (and we) shall be welcomed by these people in the eternal habitations.

Now our Lord didn't use words haphazardly. His words are meaningful and we shall do well to understand them. I have already mentioned where this word *eklipeete*, "you are going to be eclipsed" is found in other places. Let me explain a bit more in detail.

Death Likened to an Eclipse, Not an Annihilation

In Luke 22:32, where Christ is speaking to Peter, He says, "I have prayed for thee that thy faith fail not"—that thy faith be not "eclipsed," does not disappear from the scene in the thing you are endeavoring to do. And in Luke 23:45, which has to do with the crucifixion of our Lord, where it says, "And

53

the sun was darkened," that word "darkened" is the same Greek word "eclipsed."

Now did the sun cease to exist? No, the sun was there, but it did not appear to human vision. That is what the word means. It refers to the time when you and I are no more, when we shall be eclipsed, when we will no more be seen by our fellow human beings. It doesn't mean that we shall cease to be. We will still exist.

But where do we go? It says here that those whom we have won to Jesus Christ, those whom we have made our friends, will welcome us, will receive us in "the eternal habitations," the eternal tents. Let's look at that word "tents." It is exactly the same word as we find in Matthew 17:4, describing what took place when our Lord was transfigured. You remember that Peter said, "Lord, it is good for us to be here: if thou wilt, let us make here three tabernacles; one for thee, and one for Moses, and one for Elias." "Tabernacles" is the word "tents," actual tents, *skeenas*.

Our Body Is Only the "Tent" of Our Personality

Now, very interestingly, our body is described as a tent in which our real self, our personality, dwells. Our personality is not our body. That is the shell. Our personality is that invisible essence that God has put within us that gives us life. When the personality leaves the body, that body is only good for the funeral parlor and burial under the ground. That is not our personality. Our soul, our spirit, has form that has the ability to think and feel. That is our personality. And the body is called a "tabernacle," a "tent," *skeenee*.

"Eternal" Does Not Mean "Time that Never Ends"

The word *aioonious*, "eternal," is the word that appears in a most important text of the Bible, John 3:16: "For God so loved the world, that he gave his only begotten Son, that whosoever believeth in him should not perish, but have everlasting [eternal *aioonion*, accusative case of *aioonios*] life." What is that eternal life? Because our minds are so embedded in thinking only in the realm of time and space, when we hear the word *aioonios* "eternal, everlasting," we have the idea that reference is made only to time that never ends. It is unfortunate that the translators of the New Testament have in many instances translated *aioonios* as "everlasting" implying only length of time. But really this is not the true meaning of the word. It actually refers, not to time, but to the essence of its character—constant, abiding. What kind of life is it? If you will look at Romans 16:26, for instance, you will find that it refers to God: He is called "the everlasting [or eternal] God." Now what does that mean? Does it refer to the God who never ends, whose life is everlasting? But God in Himself is that. It describes the quality of deity. James gives an excellent description of the essence of God when he says: "with whom is no variableness, neither shadow of turning" (James 1:17b). Actually what it refers to is the spiritual essence of God, the eternal God, God who is not matter, God who is Spirit. It is not necessarily speaking here about the length of the life of God. God has neither beginning nor end. It speaks of the essence of deity, the quality of deity, which is a spiritual quality. That God is eternal does not refer simply to His everlastingness, but to God being Spirit. And when reference is made to eternal life, it is not primarily the length of life that is referred to, but the quality of life. It is the same life as that which pertains to God. When you believe, when you receive Jesus Christ, you receive life that is not simply human but eternal; it is the life of God in you.

We have seen that the word "habitations" in the expression "eternal habitations" refers to "tents." A tent is indicative of a physical dwelling place. The question is whether heaven, where believers go after they die, is actually a place. We have every indication that it is. But don't ask me to describe it. You can find its description in Revelation 21:10-27.

Our Lord says that you and I are going to have a tent in which to dwell in a place such as this, a physical place.

Could it be that you and I are going to have what Paul terms a "spiritual body" capable of heavenly pleasure? I have no doubt in my mind that this is so, and as we study the other parable in Luke 16 of the Rich Man and Lazarus, we become aware of the reality of existence in the world to come. It is worth any sacrifice here on earth to know that the glory of the future may be yours and mine. Eternal habitations are the habitations that God has prepared for the believers.

Everlasting Life Not Promised to Unbelievers

I heard a radio message the other day in which the speaker said that unbelievers are going to have everlasting life. Continuous conscious existence, yes, but you never find in Scripture that "everlasting or eternal life," *aioonios zooee,* is promised to an unbeliever. An unbeliever does not have the life that proceeds from God, eternal abundant life that gives peace to the heart. This is the basic meaning of the word *aioonious,* "eternal."

Is Heaven a Physical Place?

Now, if *aioonious* refers to the essence of God, and *skeenai* refers to tabernacles or habitations—tents, meaning something physical,—and if the Lord is speaking of this steward as a type of those who acted wisely in this life by giving their money so that souls might be won to Christ and be friends of theirs and friends of the Lord who would welcome them in the eternal habitations, what kind of world were they going to enter? Will it be a really physical, discernible place? I believe it will.

Turn to the 14th chapter of the Gospel of John and let me translate for you from my Greek New Testament the words that came out of the mouth of our Savior. Only a person in need of pyschiatric attention, or God in the flesh, could speak thus prior to His death about what He was going to do afterward: "Let not your heart be troubled: believe in God and believe also in me." Observe verse 2: "In my Father's house . . . ." What is there? In your English translation it says "many mansions." In the Greek it is *monai,* a word that Greeks often use today for a "monastery." *Monee* (singular nominative), "monastery," that is where the word comes from. It is a place where you stay and don't move. The verb is *menoo,* "to dwell, to inhabit." Very interestingly, however, the word *monos* related to *monee* means "alone or individual," a conclusion to which you can never arrive as you read your English translation, but which is clearly seen in the Greek text. *Monos* is derived from *memona* the perfect middle of *menoo,* to remain (Greek and English Lexicon by John Parkhurst).

It refers to a place in the house where there is an apartment, so to speak, an individual location for you.

How good to know that an individual place is reserved for each of us in Heaven. May God give us the joyous expectation of that which is yet to come.

THINK IT OVER

1. How did our Lord indicate that death was not annihilation

of conscious existence?

2. Does "eternal life" refer merely to life without end, or does it also have a deeper significance? Explain.

3. Will unbelievers have "everlasting life," in the essential meaning of that term? Explain.

4. On what do you base your hope of "eternal life"? (See John 3:36.)

8

There's a Place in Heaven Already Prepared for You

At our Lord's Last Supper with His disciples, as recorded in the 13th chapter of John, He told them that He was going to depart from this earth, and indicated who was going to betray Him. Then, in verse 33, He told them something that really disturbed them; "Where I go, ye cannot come." What was He really saying? That they could not come at that particular time. They were anxious, and their reaction was, "If you are going to go, we will come with you." But He said, "You cannot come now."

God's Timetable Unchangeable and Perfect

God has His appointed time. No one can change His timetable. As we read the Scriptures, this is one of the basic elements that we discover. There was a timetable for Jesus to come to this earth as the incarnate Son of God. There was a timetable for the Holy Spirit to come at Pentecost, in the way He came, with consequences that shall never be identically repeated. Jesus had His timetable for infilling His disciples with the Holy Spirit, but that was different. He had His timetable for leaving them so that the Holy Spirit might come in His stead. And looking at them He said, "I go, but you cannot come now." But they could come later.

And Peter, of course, always anxious to learn, said to Him, "Lord, where are you going?" (v. 36). Just like a youngster who asks, "Daddy, where are you going?" And Daddy says, "You can't come with me." We often are worse than children when it comes to our dealings with God. We want explicit answers, and we want them now. But God knows that our minds are too small to understand His reasons and purposes. As earthly parents we don't always take the trouble to tell our children what we are about to do, because we know it is beyond their comprehension. And in His wisdom, God has a right to refuse us an answer in the way we want it.

"Where are you going?" insisted Peter. And again the Lord said, "Where I go you cannot come now." Observe the word "now." You cannot *now* follow Me, but *later.* He gave specific times. And those prophets that set times are false prophets. Not now, later; leave the time to Me. You will follow Me. And Peter said to Him, "Lord, why can't I follow you now? My life I will lay down for you."

Then we come to the marvelous 14th chapter of John, one of the most revealing portions of the New Testament. "Let not your heart be troubled," said Jesus. It was because of this earthly trouble they knew they were going to experience with the departure of the Savior that they were concerned.

Heaven Is a Definite Place, Where Believers Will Have Recognizable Forms and Personalities

Now look at verse 2, "In my Father's house . . . ." A great house, with many habitations, many individual—call them apartments, call them places—for individual persons. "In my

60

father's house are many habitations: otherwise I would have said to you I go [look how easily He says it] to prepare a place for you." What does He call it? "A place." *Topon* (accusative singular of *topos*) is the Greek word. There is no doubt that this is a definite place. Our Lord who made it knows where it is. On leaving this earth, the believer is not going to be simply an idea, an invisible spirit. When you go, you are going to a place. You are going to have an essence or form that will be recognizable as you.

We all know, of course, that our resurrection bodies will be given to us when the day of resurrection comes—first to the believers and then to the unbelievers. But what happens immediately after you die? Our Lord says, "When you die, they will welcome you to eternal habitations," and He doesn't indicate any lapse of time. We all want to know what happens to a loved one when he dies. My wife will know what happens to me when I die. I will still be Spiros Zodhiates. Where will I be and what kind of a wrapping will I have? Well, we have indications in the Word of God concerning that, but I want you to note that our Lord says that it's going to be a place that you and I are going to occupy, and therefore we will not be formless disembodiments.

In the 16th chapter of Luke, in the story of Lazarus and the rich man, we have a description of how people act, what they feel, whether they can think, remember, speak, and see in the afterlife. And we will see that it is all a reality. I can't wait for it, can you? Let us thank God for this place prepared for us, in which we will not be mere indiscernible spirits, but where our personality is going to be preserved. You remember that the form and personality of Moses came back to earth on the Mount of Transfiguration—an indication that we too will have personality and form after death.

Now, the Greek word for "place" in John 14:2, *topon*, has

its English derivative in the word, "topography." A topographer is one who describes and maps the surface of a given region or place. Two words make up this compound one. *Topos* means "place," and *graphoo* means "to write." A topographer is one who delineates the exact places belonging to a region. There is no doubt whatsoever that the word *topos*, "place," means exactly what it says. Jesus says, "I am preparing a particular place for each one of you."

Will Every Believer Have an Equally Grand Habitation in Heaven?

I wonder, is every place in heaven going to be the same? Does everybody on this earth dwell in the same kind of house? Some Christians dwell in very luxurious homes, and others in very humble ones. The poor are not always free to choose where they shall live, but the rich can choose to dwell in a $200,000 house, a $50,000 house, or a $30,000 or a $20,000 house, or even to rent a humble apartment.

I will never forget a visit my wife and I paid to a dear woman who was bedfast. Her suffering was instrumental in opening India to us to preach the Gospel. She had been mugged by thugs as she was going up to her apartment and was found on the steps with many bones broken. She was taken to the hospital, and the next day my wife and I visited her. There we met an Indian doctor who attended her floor, and I introduced the doctor to this injured woman, Janet Shoppis, and asked him to take care of her. As a result of this contact with that Indian doctor, all India has opened to us for a truly effective ministry.

After her discharge from the hospital, we visited that woman in a very poor tenement on 44th Street in New York City. And I will never forget her reply to my question, "How are you, Aunt Jeanie?"

"Oh, it is wonderful!" she said. "I am having tremendous entertainment." You might think she was referring to television. Not at all. You know what her entertainment was? She said, "I am having such fun watching the mice play with each other."

Now, why was she living in a tenement full of mice, and yet not uttering a single complaint? That is the woman who paid my fare to come back from Greece when I went there to distribute fifteen tons of New Testaments. I didn't have the fare back, and she sold all her belongings to do that for the Lord.

Now, do you think she is going to have the same mansion in heaven as somebody who sought the greatest possible luxury on earth? I don't believe it. I believe the Lord is building you and me an apartment, the luxury of which is in inverse proportion to the luxury in which we chose to dwell on earth. He is going to prepare a place. What kind of place? It all depends on the materials that you and I send to heaven aforetime. A word to the wise is sufficient.

Proof of the Deity of Jesus Christ

Now, let's look a little further at John 14:2: "In my Father's house are many mansions" (or individual dwelling places, let's call them), and then Jesus says, "I go . . . ." Just the word *poreuomai*, "I go," means "I take a walk." So common a word to describe His going from earth to heaven, I don't know how many millions or billions of miles. To Him it was just like you and me taking a walk from one house to another. "I go!" Whoever says that Jesus never claimed to be God should look at this verse. "I take a walk to heaven." Why was He going? "To prepare"—and that is a once-and-for-all event, the infinitive of the aorist tense—"I go to prepare a place [*topon*] for you." He had said in the first verse, "Let not your hearts be troubled, but believe in God and believe also in me." Did Jesus ever claim to be God? What else can you make of these words: "The same faith that you exercise in God the Father, exercise in Me also," not a different kind of faith.

And then He says in verse 3, "And if I go and prepare...." Now it is very interesting that the verbs used here in the Greek text are in the aorist subjunctive tense. "And if I go ....," meaning "I am going once now." The Lord Jesus is not keeping a shuttle between heaven and earth.

Why Hasn't Jesus Returned to Earth in Answer to Our Fervent Prayers?

Some people want Jesus to come back immediately, but He has a timetable that is absolutely inviolable. No matter how much we pray, "Lord Jesus, come"—and this prayer has been prayed by all the ages of believers, from John as a prisoner on the Island of Patmos until now—He still has not come. Doesn't He hear us? Why doesn't He come? There is one simple answer: the Lord Jesus has a timetable that is eternal and He will keep it. There are certain conditions that must first be fulfilled, and when He sees them fulfilled He will come.

He says, "And if I go [that is in the aorist indicative of a once-and-for-all action] and prepare [again the aorist] a place for you...." Do you think that all the Lord Jesus Christ is now doing is preparing places for us? He has done it already. It is up there. He can do with one word what it would take a whole universe ages and ages to do. He created the world in the first place. Observe, He doesn't say, "I shall create a place." It is already created. He is simply, if I may use a mundane term, "furnishing it for us." And if someone said to me, "Do you think that in heaven I am going to have only the secondhand furniture that I have had in my life as a preacher of the Gospel?" I would assure him that he will get only the best. And in contrast to your sacrificial way of life, Jesus is preparing something wonderful for you. The more you sacrifice for Him down here, the greater things you will have prepared for you to enjoy throughout eternity. He went back to heaven, not to create, but to prepare.

Our Resurrection Bodies Will Be Like Christ's

It is all there; and the apartment, the furnishing, the comfort that you are going to enjoy, in a resurrection body like that of the body of Jesus Christ, is waiting for you. It will be a spiritual body, not restricted to the present laws of time and space or the present material world, and yet capable of enjoying not only what we are enjoying down here on earth but far more. The Lord Jesus' resurrection body went through closed doors. He traveled any space that He would without having to go step by step. He was not restricted by material space, and yet He enjoyed His breakfast on the shore of the Sea of Galilee after His resurrection. Yes, He was unrestricted, capable of enjoyment of these material comforts. Of course, the material comforts will be of a little different nature than those we have today, yet we see here that he is going to prepare for us a place. He is there waiting for us, and all is ready for us to enjoy in His presence. May our Lord help us to view this temporary world and life in view of what is yet to come.

Who Can Tell Us for Sure What Happens After Death?

No scientist can tell us what is going to happen to us when we die. There is only One Person who knows, and that is the

Lord Jesus Christ, who proved that He knew what He was talking about, because He not only foretold His resurrection but came back from the dead. Therefore, He is the best source of information as to what happens to you and to me as believers. He told us that at death we are going to go to a place He has prepared for us, to live eternally with those of like precious faith in the presence of the Godhead.

How Can We Be Sure of Christ's Return?

Now either Jesus told the truth or He is a deceiver. One of the two—and He never told a lie. He kept every promise He gave. So when in John 14:3 He says, "I come again," we can be sure He will keep that promise, too. Very interestingly He does not say, "I will come again," but "I come," in the present tense. Now why did He say that? No doubt that we would be prepared for His coming at any time.

You know, in the parables we are dealing with in this series of studies you find that our Lord always came back to receive an accounting of all that the people did, but He did not tell them exactly when he was coming back. And He doesn't want us to know the exact time of His return so that we will always be in readiness instead of waiting till the eleventh hour. "I come," or "I am coming again," is actually what He said. And the next verb is in the future tense: "And I shall receive you unto myself, that where I am you also may be." How interesting that though the Lord was speaking these words while He was still on earth, He says, "that where I am," referring to His being in heaven. Simultaneously, while the Lord was speaking these words in His incarnate God-man essence on earth, He was also in heaven, and He is there at this time. He has a place ready for you and for me, and He is coming back to receive us unto Himself.

Then in verse 4 He says, "And where I [myself] go . . . ."

The word "myself," *egoo,* is the "ego," you know. The Lord often used the words "I myself," but nobody could call Him an egotist. You could call Him God, but not an egotist. "Where I [myself] go, you know . . . ."

Now the word "know" in the Greek text there is *oidate,* which refers to intuitive knowledge, not acquired knowledge. "You know that I am going," said Jesus in effect, "not because that knowledge has come to you from anybody else, but because of your relationship to Me. You know that when you die you are going to be with Me."

Now my child knows that I love him because of his relationship to me; and the only way a human being can know where he is going after death is as a result of his relationship to Jesus Christ. There is no other way. If that knowledge came merely as a mental acquisition, it would do him no good on his deathbed. It is that relationship that exists between you and God, that you are a child of God, that brings the certain knowledge that when your body is laid in the ground you are not finished. You are with Jesus.

What Is Meant by Dwelling in Tents: Here and Hereafter?

There is an interesting passage also in II Peter 1:13 and 14. I will quote it from the Amplified New Testament, which makes the meaning crystal clear: "I think it right, as long as I am in this tabernacle [tent, body], to stir you up by way of remembrance; since I know that the laying aside of this body of mine will come speedily, as our Lord Jesus Christ made clear to me." Compare Luke 16:9, "They shall welcome you in the eternal tents, in the eternal habitations." Now the body is called in Scripture a tent, exactly the same word, and Peter says here that he is "in this tent." You have a tent in this life, and that is your body. In other words, you, your real

67

personality, now dwells in one kind of tent, but when you go beyond death you are going to find another tent, another body, in which you are going to dwell. That body, as this one, has form and shape. It may be better looking than yours or mine now, and of a little different disposition. I hope so, at least as far as I am concerned. There is a tent awaiting us, another body, that the Apostle Paul calls a spiritual body, in heaven.

Praise God that we can look forward to that new body, that new tent in which our real personality will dwell. How thankful we are that death does not end all. God help us to use our present tent, our present body, with fear and trembling, in view of the one that is coming.

THINK IT OVER

1. Is heaven a definite "place"? What words does Jesus use to enable us to answer this in the affirmative?
2. Cite proofs of Jesus' claim to be God in this parable and in its relation to John 14:1-4.
3. Why doesn't Jesus answer our prayers for a quick return? How can we be sure He *will* return?
4. What is meant by dwelling in "tents," here and hereafter?

9

Dealing Wisely
With Life's Mysteries

Now let's turn to Luke 16:10, and continue our Lord's parable about the faithful steward. He says, "He who is faithful in the smallest thing is faithful in much: and he who is unjust in a small thing or in the least thing is unjust in much." Then He goes on to tell us what constitutes a faithful steward.

What Constitutes a Wise Steward in the Eyes of Our Lord?

Notice that He calls this man a steward repeatedly, in verses 1, 3, and 8. In this connection, you will recall another important parable of our Lord's about the faithful and the wise stewards. This is found twice—in Matthew 24:45-51 and Luke 12:42-53. Notice also that these two words—faithful and wise—are used in the 16th chapter of Luke as well.

Let's just look at this other parable, because the two are very closely connected. In Luke 12:41 we read, "Then Peter said unto him, Lord, speakest thou this parable unto us, or even to all?" Of course, he was referring to the previous parable.

Now look at verse 42, "And the Lord said, Who then is that faithful and wise steward, whom his lord shall make ruler over his household?" Note three words here: "steward," which is *oikonomos,* from which "economy" is derived; "faithful," which is *pistos,* exactly the same word that we find in the 16th chapter of Luke; and "wise," *phronimos.*

Let's examine that last word. There are two Greek words for "wise": *sophos,* from which the name Sophie comes. *Sophia* means "wisdom," and when it's a name of a girl it means "wise girl." If you have that name, you should try to live up to it! However, another Greek word, *phronimos,* is also translated "wise." This is the word used both in the 16th chapter of Luke and the 12th chapter of Luke in the parable of the faithful and wise steward. These three words are most important and we are going to examine them carefully.

Are You "Pulling on the Oars" or Just Drifting Along?

First of all, we note that the Lord calls His servants "stewards." In I Corinthians 4:1 and 2 the Apostle Paul writes (and I am translating directly from my Greek New Testament) "Thus let every man consider you [take account of you] as servants of Christ." The word "servants" there is *hupeeretas,* "under-rowers." In a boat, the people on top give directions, while those who are actually doing the work are the "under-rowers," *hupeeretas,* "servants," not bond slaves. That is what you and I are, and people are watching us to see whether we are actually pulling on the oars, doing some hard work, in the Kingdom of God. That is the first thing.

In this first verse, Paul mentions two facets of discipleship: "servants" and "economists or stewards of the mysteries of God." And in verse 2 he goes on to say, "And what is that which is sought from the economists, from the stewards? That each one be found faithful." The Lord requires each disciple of His to be first *hupeeretees* (singular), "a servant," and second "a steward who is a dispenser of the mysteries of God." Now what are these mysteries of God that we are supposed to dispense to the world? Before we study that, let us look at some of the mysteries of God's providences in our own lives, and how we are to handle them.

Confronting the Mysteries of Life

What is a mystery? It is an event that seems to have no logical explanation. As we go back to this story of the rich man and his steward, we see that the Lord is calling him a faithful and wise steward because of the way he handled the mysteries of life. Put yourself in his place. To the steward it was a mystery why he was dismissed. Here he was doing his best, giving all his time, probably working overtime, and apparently not being paid for it, because when he was about to be dismissed from his job, he didn't have any money. He had no friends either, and he confronted a second mystery: "What am I going to do now that I am being dismissed from my job?" This is a very practical problem that our Lord brought up, for we are going to meet similar situations in our own lives. We may have superiors who are not appreciative of our work. And whether we like it or not, this is one of the greatest mysteries of the Christian life. We may be doing our best, yet not be adequately appreciated.

That was the case with this man. He worked hard, yet he was unjustly fired, "Now what am I going to do now that my employer is dismissing me from my job, and I have no friends and no money? Here I have been honest and never stolen anything, and look how he is treating me." And our Lord is equating that situation, the steward's dismissal, with death, with *metastasis,* you remember.

71

The Mystery of Undeserved Suffering

Sooner or later you and I are going to look upon life and confront the mystery of undeserved suffering. A little child may be taken away from us, a husband snatched away from a wife, or a wife from her husband. The most loving and saintly person you ever knew may suddenly be taken away, and you say, "Lord, why did you do it? Why didn't you take a bum? Why did you take my husband? Why did you take my child? Why did you do this to me?" These are the unanswerable mysteries of life, not merely to be dismissed from your job, not only to be unappreciated by your superiors, but *metastasis,* the taking away of a loved one from this life.

How to Be a Good Steward of the Mysteries That Throw Your Life into Turmoil

Are you a good steward of situations like that? How are you viewing them? Someone asks you for an explanation. You don't have one. No matter how hard you try to explain the mysteries of life as ordained or permitted by God, there is no adequate explanation. How could Bach explain his blindness or Beethoven his deafness? And yet had it not been for the necessary discipline that resulted from their infirmities, their talents might have never been fully harnessed for the benefit of our world.

But this man was found to be a faithful steward, not because he fought with his boss, not because he tried to restore himself to his position, but because he accepted the inevitable and said, "What do I do now?" And he did something about it. He found two bad debtors of his lord and he forgave them part of their debt, maybe collected the balance for his boss, and made friends. This is a true illustration of prudence. You may find yourself being hurt by a human boss. You feel that God is unjust to you. What do you do? Do you fight with the unjust boss or with a Sovereign God? Mind you, I didn't say an unjust God, for God always acts in the context of His plans for the total universe, not just for you and me. But God acts also in view of your eternal good, not always your temporary good. God acts in view of infinity. We look at the situations within the context of the here and now. He looks upon the whole world. He looks upon your whole life, not only your temporal life, but upon your eternal life, your forever life, and He acts accordingly.

What are you going to do? Who is a wise steward of this life? Are you going to fight against the boss that is unjust to you? Are you going to constantly complain against God because your *metastasis,* or the death of another, has come upon your family, and you consider this most unjust? Or are you going to accept it and say, "What am I going to do now that my economy is removed from me?" Suppose you lose everything, all your money and family, like Job. What do you do? Shoot your brains out? No! There is always a way out. Accept the mystery and take it from there. This, the Lord says, is wisdom, to act as stewards of the mysteries of God. We will not always understand God's ways, but we can pray for the grace to accept them, and react by building upon the foundation of His promises never to leave or forsake us, but to see us through our troubles as faithful and wise stewards of His providences.

THINK IT OVER

1. Name two requirements of a steward—that is, two areas or facets of his ministry.

73

2. Have you encountered mysteries in your life that led you to wonder about God's dealings with you?

3. How should you confront the mystery of undeserved suffering in your life and the lives of others?

10

Wise Relationships With God and With Believers and Non-Believers

When you read the word "wise" in your English text, you do not know whether it is one of three Greek words, each of which has a significantly different connotation. We have seen that one word is *sophos* or *sophia*. The meaning of this is wisdom in its highest and noblest sense. It refers primarily to God's wisdom and to the wisdom of that capacity of the heart and mind that God Himself implants in man that enables him to behave properly toward God. We have two areas of behavior: our relationship with God, and our relationship with humanity. One who manages his life in accordance with God's requirements is *sophos*, "wise."

Wisdom in Our Relations with Other People

Now, if a person is capable of managing his affairs properly with his fellow humans, he is *phronimos*. It is impossible for us to differentiate between these two words when they appear in the English text simply as "wise." It is better, I believe, to translate *phronimos* as prudent.

Wisdom That Leads to Right Judgments but Not Necessarily Right Actions

And there is still another word, *sunetos*, referring to the person who can make right judgments without necessarily carrying them out in proper behavior. A person may know what is right and what is wrong. He may know how to treat others, but he doesn't necessarily follow that judgment. To follow out a proper judgment takes *phroneesis* (the substantive —prudence) and that is the word in its adjectival form that is used in the parable of the faithful and wise servants in Luke 12:45 and also in this parable in Luke 16.

Our Lord said that the way this steward acted was considered *phronimos*; in other words, he acted properly toward other people. He was *phronimos*, "wise," in his relationship with his job and with his boss who fired him. He made the proper judgment and he actually followed it in a practical way.

Remember "The Boss May Not Always Be Right—But Right or Wrong, He's Still the Boss!"

One of the things I believe that he made a right judgment on was the inequality between the boss and himself. The boss may not even have been as bright as his steward, leading him to think, "Why should this rich man have so much money, while I have so little? Well, he is stupid, and I am going to act smart and take advantage of him." No, the steward knew that he was his boss, and he had to treat him as such and not try to outsmart him. Now that is *phronimos*, "prudent" when you deal with other people. If you recognize the responsibilities of your position and your exact relationship to the one who is above you, you will be wise. It is not always the ruler of a country who is the most intelligent man in that country. Nor is the principal of a school necessarily smarter than the teachers under him. The same holds true of students and teachers. I remember many times in class I had teachers who were so wrong in their philosophy of life, I almost felt like putting my hands over my ears so that I wouldn't have to listen to them. But what did I do? Did I get up and say, "Hey, you stupid idiot!" That would have been imprudent. You recognize realities even while you recognize the deficiencies of others, for the Scriptures teach us that those who are over us are placed there by God for some purpose. Recognize your position, recognize the authority of the other. Don't undervalue your intelligence, but you don't have to overvalue the intelligence of your boss. However, when it comes to your relationship with him, you would be unwise to call him stupid, and say, "I quit!" Think always of the consequences of your judgment and of your actions. Be wise, don't burn your bridges behind you.

An *aphroon* person, an unwise or a non-prudent person is one who may realize something and make a correct judgment, but unwisely hastens to execute his actions before the proper time. How we need the ability to make wise judgments and carry out wise actions toward others, especially as an employee toward an employer. The employer may be intolerable, but remember he is still the boss. And this steward is called prudent because he realized this. He did not reject his boss or attack him, I am sure, even when he was fired. He simply said, "All right, what do I do now?"

May God give us the wisdom to know not only how to deal with Him as our God, but also the prudence to know how to deal with those in life who are over us and with those who are under us in our human relationships.

In concluding the parable of the rich man and his steward in the 16th chapter of Luke, Jesus said in verse 10, "He who is faithful in the least will be faithful in much; and he who is unjust in the least is unjust also in much." In other words, we will be judged as much by the little things that we do as by the big things.

But who does He refer to as being faithful? It is the steward, because it is the steward that He commended back in verse 8 for acting wisely. In other words he acted prudently as far as his relations with other people were concerned. "Wise," *sophoos* (adverb, "wisely"), as noted previously, means acting well in your relationship with God. *Phronimoos* (adverb, "prudently") means acting well in your relationship with humans. You know, there are some people who talk like saints when they commune with God, but when it comes to dealing with people, they are impossible to get along with. They may think they are saints when they are dealing with God, because they are right in their own eyes, and feel that He must agree with them. But by their actions they say, "Sure I love God, but don't tell me to say good morning to my obnoxious neighbor." That is another thing all together.

We are told that this steward was prudent in his relationship with people, and in verse 8 the Lord said to His disciples that the people of this generation are more prudent when it comes to dealing with their fellow men than even the disciples. And isn't it true? Try to get born-again believers of three or four different denominations to work together and see how much of *phroneesin* "prudence (accusative)", they exercise toward each other. But take a Jew, Greek, and a Lebanese, for instance, who go into business together to make money, and they will be in full agreement in spite of their individual differences simply because they know what the bottom line should read, profit!

78

Don't Let Denominational Differences Hinder Your Cooperation With Born-Again Believers in spreading the Gospel

Now our Lord says, "Listen, you Christians, you disciples who are saying that you want to revolutionize the world for Jesus Christ, you have an end to meet. Get your heads together despite your individual differences." Nobody can fully agree with someone else on everything. Each of us possesses an individuality, along with a certain philosophy of life, but in order to work together we do not need to have exactly the same viewpoints. And if we prayed for each other, who knows what might happen to the bottom line, the work of Jesus Christ?

Should Christians Associate Only With Christians?

Our Lord is saying here, "Examine your relationships with other people—Christians with Christians, Christians with unbelievers." Do you know where to draw the line between cooperation and compromise? There are some people who say, "I don't want to have anything to do with that guy; he is a crook." But if you don't want to have anything at all to do with him, you will never be able to influence him for Jesus Christ. Who suffers? All you're doing is inflating your saintly ego. But that man may have one last chance of knowing the grace of God through seeing your saintliness in action. If your saintliness is going to be restricted to a closet, it isn't doing anybody good, not even yourself.

Outwitted

He drew a circle that shut me out—
Heretic, rebel, a thing to flout.
But Love and I had the wit to win:
We drew a circle that took him in!

—Edwin Markham

There are other people who say, "Well, I am not going to buy anything from anybody who is not a Christian." Is that the proper attitude? Not really. Of course, you should support those who are of "like precious faith." But Galatians 6:10 tells us to "do good unto *all* men, especially [but not exclusively] unto them who are of the household of faith." Hopefully in the latter case some of the profits will go to advance the Gospel of the Lord Jesus Christ. But if you refuse to go into a restaurant because worldly people patronize it, maybe some of those people will never have a chance of seeing a person bow his head and pray, thanking God for his food, instead of going right ahead and eating it without a thought of who made it possible in the first place. Judge, be prudent, in regulating your relationship with others. This steward was said to have this wonderful grace by our Lord, and this is why the Lord says that the steward of the mysteries of God ought to be *phronimos,* (first person plural) doing what is right in his relationships with others. Otherwise, he should not claim to be a steward of the mysteries of God. He doesn't belong there. He will do more harm than good.

May God help us so to regulate our lives, not that we may have a greater idea of ourselves, not that we may keep our saintliness exclusively to ourselves, but that we may make the Christ within us contagious in the midst of those who need Him.

THINK IT OVER

1. Do you get along well with God?
2. Do you get along well with other Christians, born-again believers, and can you cooperate with them in spreading

the Gospel whether they belong to your particular denomination or not?

3. What is your attitude toward unbelievers?
   a. I shun them—
   b. I treat them as good friends, making no distinction between them and believers—
   c. I seek to win them to Christ by befriending them whenever I can, but do not go along with their wrong practices—

11

Forget the Injustices
of the Past;
Look to the Future

In I Corinthians 4:1, the Apostle Paul tells us that we, as Christians, are the servants of Christ and the economists or the stewards of the mysteries of God. And one of the things that we must realize is that we live in a world of interrelationships, and he who knows how to deal with his fellow man is prudent. This steward who was unjustly dismissed from his office behaved in an exemplary manner. He did not say to himself, "Why should some unjust man like my boss have so much and I so little?" When he left his boss's office he did not spit in his face, he did not fight with him; and when he met some of his boss's debtors he did not bad-mouth his boss to them.

The Mystery of Wealth and Power Being in the Hands of Those Who Use It Unjustly

Our Lord calls such a man a prudent man, *phroneemos*, a man who knows how to behave in a world of different people of different temperaments. It is one of the mysteries of life why some should have more than others—not only more money but also more power—and why that power should be controlled by somebody who uses it unjustly.

It hurts when you are a good worker, doing your very best for somebody, and he doesn't appreciate it. In some instances, in righteous indignation a person will turn to the government and petition them to enact a law to put such men in their place. "Take away his money and distribute it evenly. This is what should be done," is the cry of the oppressed. But remember, God did not make the whole creation uniform. Look at the trees. Are there two branches the same? Are there two leaves exactly alike? Are there two people (except, perhaps, identical twins or identical triplets) who are exactly the same in every way? Impossible. God, in His wisdom, created a world for us to live in that, while not uniform, is yet united in its differences to accomplish His purposes.

God's Creation Is Infinitely Varied, to Achieve His Over-all Purposes

A majestic exposition of this thesis by the Apostle Paul is found in I Corinthians 12, where he describes the unity in diversity of the body. You remember what he says? "The eye cannot say unto the hand, I have no need of thee." And he means that the weaker member of the body cannot say to the stronger member, "I despise you," or the stronger despise the weaker. Do you realize that you couldn't write well if it were not for that little member, your thumb?

In India recently I saw one of the children suffering from leprosy. He was being treated at one of our hospitals. Leprosy had affected the nerves of his thumb. He could not use the other four fingers. We had to first operate on his thumb and only then could physiotherapy be applied to the other fingers.

It is essential to hold all the other fingers in place when you write. God has created a world of variety. How would you like it if everybody looked alike? How could you tell who was your wife or husband? Do you think God didn't know what He was doing when He made differences in His creation, including His people?

Observe that in this 16th chapter of Luke there are two parables, both of which speak of a rich man. One had a steward whom he apparently was not paying enough. That is a mystery, isn't it? Why shouldn't everybody be paid the same? But think about it. In a world where people have a different capacity to produce, you would steal away everyone's incentive to do his or her best, and you would never have enough bread to eat, or water to drink, or clothes to wear, or houses to live in. You would exist in a completely stagnant society.

You remember how the Lord reacted to the man who hid the one pound he had been given, and wouldn't use it? Our Lord took it away from him and gave it to the servant who had produced the most. You can't escape it; it is a fact of life; we live in a world of inequalities; and it is a wise person who realizes that there are people above him, and people below him; and the way he treats those who are above him, he himself will be treated by those below him. Some are rich, some poor. You may be in the middle. There are people above, there are people below you. Should God just take a bulldozer and make everybody equal? No, for He is wisdom. He reveals His plan, He reveals Himself, and He wants us to accept things as He in His wisdom has created them.

Observe that one of the reasons this man was called prudent was that he did not revolt against his master. He accepted what he did, just or unjust. We can and should fight injustice, but we cannot change the differences in man's make-up that produces it. Only the Lord knows why He permitted this to happen in the steward's life. To seek the reason is wise, and to accept God's will in your life is wise also. We need to realize that we live in a world of inequalities, a world that can never fully please us. Yet, by God's grace we can accept that which we cannot change, and that which, in principle, has been ordained by Him. As the famous "Serenity Prayer" has it: "Lord, grant me the serenity to accept the things I cannot change; the courage to change the things I can; and the wisdom to know the difference."

One of the things that this steward prudently recognized was that there are inequalities in life. Here was a rich man, his boss, who was treating him in an unjust manner. Since there was nothing he could do to persuade him otherwise, he accepted that and tried to do something about it.

A Verse That Explains the Origin of the Inequalities of Life

In connection with that, I want to call your attention to a verse in I Corinthians 4:7: "For what [in Greek, it's not 'what' but 'who'] maketh thee to differ from another? and what hast thou that thou didst not receive? now if thou didst receive it, why dost thou glory, as if thou hadst not received it?" I love that verse because it explains to me that God is the Author of inequalities as we see them. The Apostle Paul is asking this question of those who are proud. He says, "What is it that distinguishes you or me? What is it that makes you different from others?"

Fighting to Equalize Everything in Life Is Fighting Against God's Pattern

What is it that makes people different one from the other?

Is it just the genes? Is it their environment? People fight and struggle and go to war to equalize everything in this life. Is that according to God's pattern or are we fighting against Him? I believe that our struggle to equalize everything and everybody runs contrary to God's design. If He wanted it that way, He would have made it that way.

And Paul is asking the question, "Who is it that makes thee different? And what do you have that you did not receive?" In other words, in the final analysis, there is nothing that you can take total credit for; it is of God. When you bake a fine loaf of bread, or paint a beautiful picture, or listen to a talented musician, don't give yourself or another person all the credit. Start with God. To make a loaf of bread possible, He sent the rain, and made the law of generation that caused the seed to sprout and grow into wheat to furnish bread to sustain you. Behind everything that you have, behind everything that you see, recognize God. He it is who gives you everything that you possess; "and what have you that you did not receive? And if you received it, why are you proud, as if you had not received it?" Will you please mark this as the answer to the puzzle of life's inequalities? God is the Author of them, and don't be afraid and ashamed of saying it.

How to React to Injustice

And this steward was wise. When his boss said, "You're dismissed," there was no reason for his dismissal that he could accept as valid. Yet knowing the decision would not be reversed, he accepted it. He was wise also in not fighting that decision, but in seeing what he could do about it. He began by saying, "Never mind the past; what do I do from now on?"

It is likely that any of us may meet a situation like this. What is the wise thing to do? If reason does not prevail, do you start fighting the one who has caused you the injustice and spend the rest of your life in proving him wrong? Here is wisdom. In the Word of God you will find more sociology than you could find in any textbook on the subject. Don't waste time fighting those who treat you unjustly. You will hurt yourself more than you hurt them. Stand for the truth, of course. Maintain your integrity, and that you have been wronged. But don't spend the rest of your life fighting that person, who probably will never admit or even realize he is wrong. You can't change him.

Forget the Past; Look to the Future

Be realistic. Think of yourself and the best course of action to take with regard to your future. That's what this man did as he left his boss's office. He said, "What am I going to do? How am I going to face *my* future? My boss's future has already been decided. He has done me an injustice. I believe in the justice of God, and vengeance is not mine but God's. It is my duty to see what I can do with my life from now on."

People who spend their lives in a negative attitude, fighting others all the time, are most unwise. Be realistic about others, evaluate them factually, but think constructively. Don't brood over how you can eliminate the presence of your oppressor, but concentrate on what you are going to do so that your future will be brighter than your past. That is wisdom—the wisdom of dealing with your own life and its relationship with other people.

When our Lord said in Luke 16:8 that the steward had "done wisely," the verb translated "did" that is used in the Greek text is *epoieesen*, not *epraxen*. What is the difference? *Praxis* is an act by itself, usually not a good act. To do something that is wrong we usually use the Greek word *prattoo*, meaning not too commendable, or amoral. But when it comes to doing something like taking different parts

88

of a puzzle and putting them together so that you can get the whole picture, we use the word *poieoo*, "to do." And that's the word from which we get the noun *poieema*, which means "a creature or a poem," something of beauty, something of which you have taken the various parts to make a meaningful whole. (See Luke 23:51, Acts 19:18.)

Here is a steward who took different parts of his life and made something good out of seeming misfortune. A boss, an unjust rich man who dismisses him on a rumor, resulting in poverty because he never paid him enough—"What am I going to do with all this stuff in my life?" he asks. "Am I going to just take it apart piece by piece and analyze it and say, 'Oh! that unjust guy, I hate him! Boy, I'd like to punch him in the nose!' "

Oh, no, no, no! Take life in its totality. Put the pieces of the puzzle together. Make a whole. The injustices of man, the differences that exist in the world of reality, it's up to you to make something good out of them. Make a whole, make a poem, make something of beauty to others. A person who can do that, the Lord says, is a prudent person.

Retaliation Is Futile, Harmful, and Sinful

Now, this fellow did not try to retaliate against his master. Let not that be your aim toward somebody who has done you an injustice. Nor did he go to the creditors of his lord and say, "If I were you I wouldn't pay him back one single penny. He's an unjust man, and I'm here to tell you all the truth about him."

Read the parable again. He did not say one bad word against his lord. He is wise who suffers an injustice and does not speak ill of the person who causes it. I don't believe this man had any resentment against his boss for what he did to him. The person who keeps rehearsing the resentments of the past can never deal as he should with the challenges of the present. If you hold bitterness in your heart for past injustices, you will never be able to do your present and future tasks as well as you should. Let not your creative mind dwell on destructiveness but on constructiveness. Don't think of the past and say what you could have been, but build, go forward, forget the past, and concentrate on where you desire to go. Put all your power into the present task and move forward unhindered by past resentments.

Money or Friends—When It Comes to a Choice, Which Is Most Important?

Our Lord also considered this man prudent because when it came to a choice between making money and making friends, he preferred the latter. He went out and said, "What can I do to befriend people?" He did that by forgiving them certain indebtednesses, but his aim was not to make money in the interval between the time he was fired and the time when his dismissal became effective. His aim was to make friends so that they would help him when he was in need. The most miserable person on earth is the one who has money and no friends. The person who spends all his time in making money and disregards the value of fellowship with others is decidedly not wise. Our Lord calls a person wise who considers fellowship with others more important than money. May God help us not to hold grudges or resentments, but to bury the past, to forget it, and to move forward to the victories of the future. May we realize that we are responsible for taking the pieces dealt to us in life and making something good out of them.

You know, the unjust employer may actually have done the steward a favor without knowing it. He enabled him to go out on his own and do something about his problem by collecting some bad debts by discounting them, and so making friends of these debtors. Sometimes an injustice is actually for our good. If instead of becoming bitter we take it as a challenge to do something greater or better in life, we shall eventually thank God for such an injustice.

A Personal Experience of How an Injustice Led to a Worldwide Witness for Christ

I remember when I was 16 years of age, I was thrown out of a Greek high school simply because I preached a sermon to my fellow students. The priest who was my teacher became infuriated and started to attack me in class. So I pulled out my Greek New Testament and answered him, and I told him what I knew and what I stood for. He didn't have a New Testament to counter me, but he became angry because I stood my ground.

Well, he went down to the headmaster and had me expelled, and I thought I would be an ignoramus the rest of my life. I went home and began to read a Greek newspaper, one that was received by every Greek in Cairo. And as I had plenty of time after being expelled from school, to read every page in that paper, the idea came to me—wouldn't it be wonderful to have a Gospel message in this newspaper? It would reach all the Greeks in that area—and that is when the newspaper evangelism concept was born in my heart. As a result of being thrown out of school, not because I did anything wrong, but because I witnessed for my Lord, millions and millions of people today are able to receive the Gospel in their secular newspapers in many languages and countries around the world, as a result of this injustice that was perpetrated against me.

Yes, this employer was unjust to his faithful steward, but he who receives an injustice and builds on it and takes it as a challenge is a wise man. Let us seek God's grace to use unjust actions against us as stepping stones to progress.

THINK IT OVER

1. Have you ever been treated unfairly? How did you react?
2. Is retaliation permitted to a Christian? Is he or she allowed to try to get even, or to treat others in as harsh a manner as they have been treated?
3. How should a Christian react to personal injustices? (See the Sermon on the Mount, Matt. 5:10, 11, 38-48.)
4. Is there anyone you hold a grudge against? Are you praying for that person? Would you help him or her in trouble? Does Christ require this of you?

12

Faithfulness Required
in Small Matters and Great

In Luke 16:10, our Lord said that the one who is faithful in small matters is also faithful in great ones. Now whom did He refer to as being faithful? Not to the rich man, of course, but again to the steward. The word faithful comes from *pistis,* "faith," in Greek. In this connection, it refers only to humans and their character.

In I Corinthians 1:9 the Apostle Paul also applies the word "faithful" to God: "Faithful the God through whom you were called unto fellowship with his Son, Jesus Christ, our Lord." "Faithful the God" is how the expression reads in Greek. What did Paul mean by "faithful"? Dependable. That's the word: faithful, dependable, trustworthy.

God's Faithfulness or Dependability the Norm for the Christian

And our Lord chose the same word that the Apostle Paul used to indicate God's dependability, and applied it to this steward. He who is dependable in the least thing is to be trusted for big things. He follows this up immediately with the antonym, the opposite, of faithfulness or dependability: "injustice." Observe: the faithful one, the dependable in the least, is also dependable in much; and he who is unjust, *adikos,* in the least, who does not do righteously, is unjust also in much. And, of course, how you apply this depends on your criterion of what is right and wrong. Many people who do wrong never have any consciousness of sin, because their wrong attitude, their wrong character, their wrong principle, is the standard by which they go. Unless they are convicted by the Holy Spirit, they will never know how sinful they are. The sinfulnes of sin depends on our appreciation of what is evil and what is good. So, he who does not do right in little things will not do right in great things.

Who Was Unrighteous and Who Was Wise in the Parable of the Rich Man and His Steward?

And who does our Lord refer to as unrighteous, as not doing the right thing? Undoubtedly, the rich man. Why is the steward called the faithful one, the dependable one, and the rich man called unrighteous? Well, first of all, the steward was dependable in all that he was doing while he was in the service of the rich man. His boss never had any reason to mistrust him. One of the reasons we conclude this is that at the end of his service, when he was dismissed, he didn't have anywhere to go. He had no money; he was broke. He says, "To dig, I am unable. I cannot do manual work; I'm a white-collar worker." What does all this indicate? That he did not steal anything from his master. Here he had full authority— and an economist has full authority to do whatever he wants with his master's possessions—and yet, in spite of that, he did not take advantage of it to fill his own pockets. For had he stolen, he would have said to his master, "You can dismiss me

94

anytime you want. I've got plenty of money. I don't need you anymore. I have been here long enough to make myself a nice little profit. I can manage my own affairs from now on." But this man was needy. He didn't have any friends to go to. He didn't have any money. He wasn't fitted for any other job, and he had enough self-respect not to go out and beg for money. I see him as a man of sterling character. He was fully dependable. He had executed his duties in a trustworthy manner.

But the other fellow, the rich man, is said to be unjust. Why? Well, the first thing was that he dismissed this faithful worker only on hearsay. The steward had been falsely accused to his boss of wasting his money. And the boss believed a mere rumor; he acted upon it without fully investigating the facts; and he hastily dismissed an innocent man. Our Lord calls any such man unjust. Anybody who would take such action against one of his employees on mere rumor, without fully investigating such accusations, is unjust.

The Sin of Spreading Unproven Rumors

How many of us are guilty of spreading such rumors, or believing them? Some people seem to take a delight in hearing ill of another, and spreading it as Gospel truth. We hear an evil word against our brother, and we go out and repeat it. We have no right to repeat any accusation against anyone unless we have documented proof. Any other course, our Lord considers an injustice. This is the contrast between these two men, as brought out in Luke 16:10. May we take the lesson to heart, and be not only dependable but also just. Let us never repeat accusations that we have not proven to be correct. May God forgive us if we have ever done so. Let us take the attitude of Richard Sheridan, who wrote these lines:

Believe not each accusing tongue,
As most weak people do;
But still believe that story wrong
Which ought not to be true.

That is the way of Christian charity.

THINK IT OVER

1. Why did our Lord call the steward faithful and wise?
2. Why did He call the employer unjust?
3. Have you known of any cases where false rumors have done great harm to another person—or perhaps even to yourself?
4. Have you the integrity of character to refuse to listen to or repeat unproven accusations against another, or do you lend an eager ear to gossip, willing to believe the worst?

13

God's Viewpoint
on Who is Just or Unjust

If I were to ask you to give me a definition of injustice, I wonder what you would say? It all depends on where you stand. The dictionary calls injustice "any act that involves unfairness to another, or violation of his rights." If you believe that the primary good in life is the service of self, then anything that tends to deprive you of what you consider your due, you consider unjust. I believe that this is what our Lord had in mind when he spoke of injustice. If you tend to want everything in life, including all other people, to serve you; if you consider yourself number one in life; then everything that tends to detract from your self-important status is injustice to you. We can call what you consider injustice "a relative injustice." But there must be an absolute about it that is set by God.

What is righteousness? What is justice? It would make an excellent Th.D. thesis to search the Scriptures and find out what God considers righteousness—the right thing to do. We may really want to do the right thing, but it is very elusive, very difficult, to determine what is absolute righteousness in each instance.

Protecting One's Interests Only Can Lead to Injustice Toward Others

Take this rich business man, for instance. What was it that he did unjustly? He called his business manager in and on hearsay dismissed him and never gave him a second chance. The loss of his own property was his most important consideration—self first, "My money, if this man is causing me to lose my money, he is no good. I must get rid of him." Selfish consideration, his own monetary gain, was his primary goal. And he never gave this man, even if he were wrong, a second chance to prove that he was not as bad as his accusers claimed. That is unjust: to consider only yourself, the protection of your selfish interests, without any consideration of the other person; not caring whether he is going to suffer, and suffer greatly, for a long time, simply because of your desire to protect your own interests.

Hasty Actions Often Result in Injustice

Secondly, I believe that this man was unjust because he acted only out of temporal considerations. In other words, he acted hastily. "I must cut the cord immediately with this man." He may have served him a long time. Yet he did not think of the long-range consequences of his hasty action in dismissing him. It is unjust to disregard the long-time consequences upon the lives of others as a result of your instant decisions that tend to satisfy your interests. Consider the other person. Think of what your hasty decision will cause in his life. Will it make it impossible for him ever to get another job? Many a time in my life as an executive I have had to dismiss people.

But one doesn't have to dismiss them with the idea of doing them harm forever. We can be kind, we can be considerate. That doesn't mean we should be hypocritical. But each person has his good qualities and his bad qualities, and we don't need to stress the bad qualities and ignore the good. Let's not consider only our temporary interests, but consider the long-range effect of our present decision upon the life of another.

Too Great Self-Concern Results in Injustice Toward Those Who Need Your Help

There is yet a third point I would like to consider. The rich man's greatest concern was self. This invariably results in injustice to others. In the Parable of the Good Samaritan, in Luke 10:30-37, we find several characters who illustrate unjust and just behavior. There was the thief who came and robbed a traveler on the road between Jerusalem and Jericho. That was an unjust act. He wanted something for himself. The traveler had it, and therefore he forceably took it away from him.That is an unjust act. To consider that you have a right to take what belongs to another simply because you need it is wrong. But the priest and the Levite who came along were just as unjust as the thief. Why? Because they came and looked at the wounded traveler but didn't help him. Their consideration was one of selfishness. Even a doctor who comes along the highway and sees an accident victim on the road may refuse to stop out of selfish considerations, lest he be involved in a lawsuit, or feels it is none of his business. If you are able to help someone, but your primary consideration in life is self, you will undoubtedly end up doing acts of injustice. So don't try to do away with the injustices of life— just do away with the number one character in your life— self—and you will become a dependable, faithful person.

Why Jesus Called the Rich Man Unjust

I believe the Lord's words in Luke 16:10 refer to the characters of the two men in the parable He has just concluded. The first half of the verse, "He who is faithful in the least, he will be faithful in much," refers, as we have seen, to the wise steward. The second half, "And he who is unjust in the least is unjust also in much," refers to the employer who treated his steward unfairly.

Now why is the Lord calling this rich man unjust? Let us look at his behavior as recorded in this parable to find out. An unjust person, *adikos* in Greek, is one who does not demonstrate righteousness. First of all he did not appreciate the hard work of his employee, the steward. Did he work hard? There is *every* evidence that he did. For we saw that when he was given his dismissal papers he said, "What am I going to do now that I am losing my stewardship? To dig, I am unable. To beg I am ashamed." This indicates that he did not have any surplus funds, and had to acquire some friends quickly who would take him into their homes when he was found in need after his dismissal. In other words, it would seem the man did not even have time for socializing, for he had no friends that he could go to. There is *every* evidence, therefore, that he had worked hard for his master, was not adequately rewarded, for he had no savings. Of course, he may have been a spendthrift, but I do not believe so for two reasons: 1) the Lord would not have called him faithful and wise; and 2) he would have had plenty of friends who had been the objects of his generosity in the past.

A Lack of Appreciation for the Good Work of Others Is a Great Injustice

No, this man's work was not appreciated or adequately

rewarded. And a lack of appreciation for those who work for us, or for those for whom we work, or for those with whom we are in any way related, is one of the greatest injustices that we could perpetrate. The spirit of not appreciating others is a selfish and uncaring character trait. Are they perfect? No one is. If ever you want to find perfection, don't look in the mirror. It doesn't reside in you, me, or anybody else. As you want others to appreciate you and your hard work, turn around and appreciate others.

This is what this rich man did not do. There is always a danger in those who have authority and affluence that they will fail to appreciate others less fortunate than themselves—those who have less wealth and influence. We must be very careful to maintain a spirit of appreciation for our fellow human beings. Remember that you and I need the least person, who does the little things of life that do not always come to our notice. Therefore our appreciation must extend to each and all, for without them we could not be what we are, or do what we do. Where would you and I be without the postman, the street cleaner, the grocer for instance? As an employer, where would we be without the person who cleans the premises, or the secretary, or clerk, or salesman who furthers our aims, and helps make our business a success? We are unjust if we do not see the good in others. Don't close your eyes to their shortcomings, but give praise where praise is due, and then when reproof is necessary, it will be accepted as your helping them to do better. Remember, God put you here, not to take advantage of others, but to help them in any way you can.

The second reason why this man was labeled unjust by our Lord is that he was too quick to believe what was said against this steward. You remember in the first verse of this parable Jesus said to His disciples, "There was a rich man who had an economist, a steward, and he was falsely accused [that is the Greek word *diebleethee,* which comes from *diabolos,* "the devil]." He falsely accused him of wasting his belongings. He called him in and fired him without examining the situation. He accepted an accusation without finding out the truth about it, and in the heat of the moment he dismissed him.

Character Assassination Is Murder. Don't Repeat Unverified Accusations.

The Lord knew how apt man is to fall into the sin of maligning others or accepting false accusations against people.Therefore He gave specific regulations against this sin in Leviticus 19:14: "Thou shalt not curse the deaf, nor put a stumbling block before the blind." Why? Because they are unable to protect themselves. Don't do anything behind somebody's back is the clear implication.

Don't forget that the worthiest persons are frequently attacked by slanderers as we generally find that to be the best fruit which the birds have been pecking at (Bacon).

This is another way in which we ourselves can be labeled unjust. When somebody says or writes something to us against someone else, let's not repeat it to anyone else. The Scripture is explicit in directing us to go to that person to confront him with the accusation, and if he does not listen, to bring him together with others to sift the matter. But unless there is absolute proof of the evil or the accusation, let's not repeat it. We must not do for another what we would not like another to do for us. Doing justice to the character of our fellow human beings should be more precious than our own lives. If I were in any way to malign a fellow human being, let alone a Christian, by saying something that I had not thoroughly checked out, I would be a murderer. I would have murdered his character, his reputation, the usefulness of his life. I am afraid there is too much of that in Christian circles. And the Lord someday will point His finger at some of us and say, "You are an unjust person."

What is justice? What is righteousness? Why would God call a human being unjust? What does he expect of a person? What does He expect of you or me?

God's Requirements for Personal Justice in the Old Testament and in the New

I believe that in the Old Testament God expected justice to be the literal fulfillment of all His commandments. And if a person obeyed the commandments of God exactly, literally as they are given, he would be considered just. In the New Testament we don't have such detailed and specific commandments about what to do and what not to do: to drink or not to drink; to eat certain foods, or to abstain; to walk or to drive two or three miles on Sunday or not to drive; how much money to spend on our house; how luxuriously we can live. All these are difficult decisions for the Christian.

In the New Testament We Are Given Basic Principles Upon Which to Form Just and Right Decisions

However our Lord gave us some basic principles in the New Testament that help us to solve these questions. He said, "Love the Lord thy God with all thy heart" (Matt. 22:37). Make your specific decisions in line with that. But He has made very clear what the consequences of our free choices will be.

For instance, in this parable we have His command to sacrifice, to spend our money for the primary purpose of leading souls to Jesus Christ. He tells us to make friends

103

through the mammon of unrighteousness—through money. And he says that the money we spend to win people to Jesus Christ will produce friends who will welcome us into the eternal habitations. They will be our welcoming committee in heaven.

Now if you believe that, you will rejoice one day to have people in heaven to welcome you, saying, "What you did down there on earth, by living in a less luxurious home, driving a less luxurious car, sacrificing in order to spread the Gospel, produced eternal results. We are the souls in heaven as a result of what you did."

Now, it is up to you whether you have one person as a welcoming committee in heaven, a hundred persons or a thousand persons; the choice is yours. The Lord wants you to know that the results will be proportional to your sacrifice. The Lord sets general principles and leaves the choice to us. The Christian religion is the one religion on this earth that allows the greatest possible freedom of choice to the individual. But if we look in the Word of God we will find that the consequences of our choices are always fixed—not in the minutest details but in general principles.

The Setting of Right Priorities Leads to Just and Proper Actions

What is right for us to do? It is right to put God first. We wouldn't be here if it were not for God. What is right? To put our parents in a very important place? The Scriptures tell us we cannot neglect them. And this responsibility also carries over to our neighbor's welfare also. God first, others second, ourselves third. If we reverse the order we are unjust in the sight of God.

The Wrong Priority of Communism: Enforced Subservience to the State

There are several political and economic systems today. A prominent one is Communism. Communism recognizes that no man can live without putting something or someone first in his life. What Communism has done is to put the state in the place of God. The state comes first, and the individual doesn't count. They force this belief upon every individual. People who live under Communism are most unhappy because of this forced subservience, and many are revolting. Communism considers a person just, righteous, as far as the state is concerned, if he gives the state first place, not out of choice, but because the state demands it.

God's Standard of Justice—Voluntary Submission to Him as Lord

God, however, considers a person just who voluntarily says, "God must come first in my life." And whatever we do in disregard of that basic consideration is injustice toward God. He who does not put God first will put himself first; and if we put ourselves and our interests first, not caring either for God or what happens to others, we are basically unjust.

To be unjust actually means to be selfish, and a selfish person cannot help being unjust in his treatment of others.

The Sin of Believing Ill of Others on the Basis of Hearsay Evidence

It is interesting to see whom the Lord calls unjust and whom He calls just. Frankly, I am fascinated by the subject. In this parable we learn it is unjust to take for granted the truth of any accusation against another person, without adequate proof. When this rich man heard the accusation against his steward, what did he do? He called only the steward into his office. "And having called him, he said unto him, What is this that I hear about you?" (Luke 16:2). You know what this man should have done? He should have called the accuser and the accused together and sat them down in his office and said, "Now I have you both in front of me. There are always two sides to every story. I want to listen to what you, the accuser, have to say, and I want to know what you, the accused, have to say."

That is how justice should work in this world. No judge can say he does justice when he calls in only the accused and says, "I have heard so and so against you; therefore, I condemn you and sentence you to imprisonment." Would you like this to happen to you, to be condemned merely on hearsay evidence? This is not justice; this is what is happening in totalitarian countries. A spy brings a charge against someone, and immediately he is sentenced or taken out to die.

Undue Consideration for Your Belongings Often Impairs Your Judgment

The wrong attitude of the rich man was that he did not call both parties to tell their story, to say what each one knew about the matter. He called only his steward and said, "What is this that I hear about you? Wasting my belongings!" Note that the emphasis is on "wasting my belongings." When your belongings are so important to you that you cannot see anything else, you will not take the time to see that justice is done. This man says, "If my money is being wasted, I am not going to tolerate anything like this. I don't have to listen to you. Where there is smoke there must be fire. Therefore, I dismiss you."

And the truth of the matter was that nothing like this had

happened, and an innocent man suffered as the result of a false accusation not fully investigated. God deliver us from such a spirit of injustice.

Now what else did this employer do that caused him to be considered unjust by our Lord? Apparently he did not offer his steward any severance pay. The man had worked hard, and all of a sudden his boss decided to dismiss him with never a thought of the effect on his future. To the rich man, the most important consideration was the prosperity of his business.

It is unjust, I believe, for any employer or for anyone else, for that matter, just to look at business, without any consideration for the individuals who are working for them or with them. It was an act of injustice on the part of the steward's employer, because he did not consider the future of this man he was dismissing.

Exercising Wisdom in Regard to Our Responsibilities to Our Work and to Those Who Work With or for Us

Now, of course, there is a very thin line of consideration here between an employer's responsibility to fulfill the task that is assigned to him and also to the individual who is working for him or with him. It takes a wise person to do his job well, and at the same time have due regard for the people who work for or with him. It is possible to do it, though of course there are some individuals who make it impossible for anybody to exercise longsuffering, understanding, and help. Some unsatisfactory, lazy, and dissatisfied workers do not want to be helped; but we will never be counted unjust if we really try the best we know how to change their attitudes, and give them a second chance. At the same time, we must keep the balance between loyalty to the task that is ours, and the responsibility to meet the needs of other human beings. We should never put a situation above a fellow human being.

107

People are more important than things. We must try to do the best we can for them and at the same time not neglect our work.

If you think that is easy, you should share my responsibility sometimes. I can fully sympathize with the responsibility of the president of a company, or the responsibilities of a pastor. They face so many conflicting elements, and must figure out how to keep the balance—not to hurt people, and at the same time to do their job well. May God give us the grace we all need in this regard. This rich man needed it very, very badly.

Give a Person a Second Chance—Just as You Would Want a Second Chance for Yourself

Another thing that I think made our Lord consider him unjust was the fact that he did not give his steward a second chance. Many a time I say to myself, "If people hadn't given me a second chance, where would I be today?" I hate to think of it; and this motivates me to turn around and say, "I must give other people a second chance, if I want others to do the same for me."

Can you imagine where you and I would be, if God didn't give us a second chance, and a third, and a fourth, and a fifth? Again we need to seek wisdom from God as to how to give a person a second chance without allowing him to destroy us or the task that we are responsible for. It is an extremely difficult problem. But deep in our hearts our motive should be, "I want to give the other person as much of a chance as I would like to have myself."

Much depends on how you give it. If you call a person in and say, "You'd better shape up, because this is the last chance I am giving you," you will never secure his willing cooperation. The way to do it is to create the circumstance and the climate that will motivate the person to respond in a positive manner. In other words, don't decide that he is going to fail as a result of the second chance before you give it to him.

This rich employer was unjust because he failed to give his steward, who had really served him well, a chance to prove that the accusation was not correct. May we have the disposition of our Lord in considering others and giving them a second chance, or many more chances, if warranted.

THINK IT OVER

1. Does everything have a dollar sign on it in your relationship with others; if a relationship hurts your pocketbook, do you break it off without regard for the other person involved?

2. Are you given to making hasty decisions that adversely affect the lives of others?

3. Are you reluctant to get involved when someone needs help, because it may cause you some inconvenience?

4. How do God's requirements for personal justice differ in the Old Testament and the New?

5. To be just one must (check those with which you agree)
   a. Hear both sides of a story.
   b. Ask for documentary proof or credible witnesses on both sides.
   c. Decide the rights and wrongs of the situation in your own mind, and act without taking time you feel you can ill afford to dig deeper into the evidence.
   d. Be willing to give a person a second chance if he is willing to try again.

14

Other Examples of People Whom God Considered Unjust

In Luke 16:8, you remember, we read the term "the steward of injustice or unrighteousness," in which we said that injustice or unrighteousness there stands for money. The Lord called it that because most people use it unjustly for selfish purposes. Then we read in verse 9 of "the mammon of unrighteousness or injustice," which is the god of money. Now in verse 11 we read of "the unjust mammon." That is the exact translation from the Greek. Jesus calls the god of money unjust.

I have looked into my Greek concordance to find out in what other places we find the expression "unjust." And I am discovering some very interesting things. If you will turn to the 13th chapter of Luke, you will find a similar expression in verse 27: "laborers or workers of unrighteousness or injustice" ("workers of iniquity" in the King James Version). It's exactly the same word as in Luke 16:11. Now who are these whom our Lord calls "the workers of injustice"? We must begin at Luke 13:22 to see what the description is all about. Let me translate these few verses for you and we will discover who these workers of injustice or of unrighteousness are.

"And he [Jesus Christ] was going about the cities and the small towns, teaching and walking toward Jerusalem. And one said to him, Lord, are the saved ones few? And he said unto them, Strive to enter through the narrow gate, because many, I say unto you, shall seek to enter, and they shall not be able to."

The Popular Notion of Salvation Versus Jesus' Stricter Requirements

Now what is going on here? What is this all about? A man asks Jesus if there are many who are saved. The people thought, of course, that a great many would be—even those who just mentioned the name of Christ. But Jesus says no, the entrance through which one must walk to be saved is not a wide one; it is very narrow. In other words being saved is not as easy as strolling down a wide boulevard.

Now go to verse 25: "And when the master of the house [or rather the despot of the house, *oikodespotees*— in other words, the person who lets people into heaven] shall rise, and shall close the door, and you will stand outside, and you will knock at the door, saying, Lord, Lord, open to us; and he answering will say, I don't know you, where you are from."

Now observe here the teaching that there are some people who think they are going to get to heaven and just walk in and get a hearty welcome. But our Lord says that's not the way it is. When they knock at the door, the doorkeeper will say, "I have never known you." And then they will begin to say, "We have eaten before you and we have drunk" (v. 26). In other words, "Don't you remember us? Every time there was something doing in church and there was food, we were there. At those potluck suppers, we were there. Don't you remember us? Open up. We ate and drank with you, and in the public squares you taught us."

And the Lord will say, "Sorry; I don't know you," and the word "know" there is *oida*, "have intimate relationship with you." Jesus will say, "I tell you, I do not know where you are from. You are not related with me. Get away from me, all ye the workers of injustice or unrighteousness" (v. 27).

Changed Lives the True Evidence of Salvation

Who are these people? Those who raise their hands when the invitation is given and say, "I accept Christ," but whose lives are never changed. They go their way, and their god is the almighty dollar. It isn't God, it is "the mammon of unrighteousness." There is absolutely no evidence of change in their lives. They come to our churches, eat in our churches, sit in the pews, listening but never doing. They are somehow given the idea that they are Christians because they have made a public profession; but there was no reality behind it. And the outside world looks at them and says, "If that is Christianity, I want no part of it."

Or they are deceived into thinking, "That is the easiest thing in the world. Here goes my hand; I will become a Christian, too." But they go right on in their own sinful ways; their heart is never changed. God is not their God. "Unrighteousness, money, injustice is their God. That's why the Lord called these people the "workers of injustice, of unrighteousness."

One of the best ways to test the genuineness of our salvation is to find out whether the old nature within us responds when it is called by an outside voice. A French woman was being sought by the police. As soon as she descended from a train a policeman approached her to ask her who she was and from where she was coming. She gave him false information and she kept on going. Then a voice was heard behind her: "Rosine." That was her real name. She immediately turned. Are you responding to the hypocritical name of a Christian in Church and in the world by your real name?

The Unjust Judge, and Why Jesus Called Him So

We find another example of an unjust person in Luke 18:6, where a judge is described by that term. The parable concerns a widow who had a complaint, and went to a judge to have it rectified; but the judge wouldn't listen.

In verse 6 we read, "And the Lord said, Hear what the judge of injustice saith." What a commentary on one who was appointed to uphold the law, that he should be called "the judge of injustice" as the Greek text has it. I am afraid there are many like him today.

First of All, He Did Not Fear God

What did this man do that caused our Lord to call him "the judge of injustice"? If you examine the story you will find that this poor widow came persistently to ask him to intervene, but he wouldn't do it. The character of this judge is given in verse 4, where he brazenly admits, "I do not fear God, and I am not ashamed before man." He was called "the judge of injustice" because of these two character traits. The fact that he would not attend to the needs of this widow was only a symptom of his character.

First of all, he was not fearful or respectful of God. Any person who does not fear God cannot possibly be just toward his fellow man. That is the conclusion, isn't it? And the unfortunate thing is that many people who don't fear God are trying to institute social justice, causing all kinds of trouble in the world. Would to God that one basic requirement for the

114

appointment of any judge would be an affirmative answer to the question, "Do you believe in God? Do you fear God?" The person who does not fear God may perpetrate injustices without any scruple of conscience. Unconsciously he makes himself God, in deciding the destinies of men.

There is no person in whose life there is no God. Either it is God out there, who is omnipotent, whom a person fears and respects, and believes he is answerable to, or he is his own god. One of the two. You know why we don't have justice in the world? It is because we have judges who don't fear God. Crime would be reduced to a minimum if they did, for enforcement of the law has to start with the judge.

Secondly, He Had Lost His Sense of Shame Toward Mankind

The second reason this judge was unworthy of his office was his declaration, "I am not ashamed of man." I believe one of the greatest curses of our society today is that man has lost the sense of shame. This leads a person to do wrong and then to say, "That is not wrong. That is perfectly all right if it serves my purposes. I don't care what others think." And I really believe that this man who is called the judge of injustice gives us a true insight into what the Lord considers an unjust person: the person who does not fear God and who is not ashamed, no matter what his conduct is toward his fellow human beings.

Thirdly, He Refused to Help the Poor and Needy When He Had the Power to Do So

Although the judge in the parable did not fear God and was not ashamed before his fellow man, the real reason he was called "the judge of injustice" was that he did not render help to a helpless creature. This poor widow had no way of securing her rights. Apparently she had some financial difference with other people. I do not know what that difference was, but she went to the judge and said, "Please take my part in standing up for my rights, for that which is due me. Defend me." And he refused. Anyone who is able to help the helpless, and refuses to do it, is an unjust person. He does not give.

Our Rights as a Citizen and Our Rights as a Child of God

Actually, when you come to the meaning of the word "unjust," *adikos,* or "unrighteousness," *adikia,* you find they both stem from the basic Greek word *dikee,* "right, justice." They refer to that which is right for oneself. We speak of our rights, that which should come to us because of what we are, because of placing ourselves under a certain regime. An American citizen for instance, has certain rights. His rights are not the same as those of a Pakistani citizen, for instance, who may be here on a visit. Our rights are determined by what we are, and by the privileges that the state, our family, our community, the social environment in which we live have given us.

God also gives a person certain rights. If you are a child of God, born again by the Spirit of God, the Word of God tells you that you can come to God in prayer boldly.

And a destitute, helpless creature such as this poor widow had certain rights also—rights given to her by God, rights granted to her by the society in which she lived, rights that were hers by virtue of the very condition in which she was found. And she went to a judge, who was in a position, and whose actual duty was, to avenge her. Yet he refused to do it.

116

Sins of Omission Are as Unjust as Actual Murder, Theft, or Adultery, in God's Sight

Many times we think that unjust people are those who actively perpetrate evil against others, hurting and harming them. That is, of course, positive injustice. But there is also the negative injustice of refusing to do for others what they cannot do for themselves, which is their rightful due, and which lies in our power to do for them.

Of course, God does not expect us to do that which is not in our power to do. But the help that this widow was asking from this judge was not only in his power, but was, in fact, his duty to do. He comes under the condemnation of James 4:17, "He that knoweth to do good, and doeth it not, to him it is sin." What is sin? Missing the mark. What is missing the mark? Refusing or avoiding the duty that you are called upon to perform.

Sin is not limited to murder, theft, or adultery. Sin is also looking at somebody who has had an accident on the road and not stopping to help him. The sin of the priest and the Levite, in the Parable of the Good Samaritan, was that when they saw the man wounded by thieves they would not stop to help him, though they were well able to do so. They missed the mark. And God considers you an unjust person if you are able to help a helpless creature like this widow in the parable, and do not do so.

Knowing How to Differentiate Between Those Who Are Helpless and Those Who Can Help Themselves

Mind you, you must always differentiate, as the Greeks did, between *penees* and *ptoochos*. *Penees* means the person who can help himself, and *ptoochos,* which is many times translated "beggar," as in Luke 16:20, means "poor, unable to help himself." You are wise if you know how to differentiate between the person who can help himself and the person who will suffer loss, or even death unless you help him, if it lies within your power to do so.

If I should see
A brother languishing in sore distress,
And I should turn and leave him comfortless,
When I might be
A messenger of hope and happiness—
How could I ask to have that I denied
In my own hour of bitterness supplied?

If I might share
A brother's load along the dusty way,
And I should turn and walk alone that day,
How could I dare—
When in the evening watch I kneel to pray—
To ask for help to bear my pain and loss,
If I had heeded not my brother's cross?

—Author Unknown

Giving In Just to Get Rid of a Person Without Regard to the Merits of the Case, Is Sin

Now look at Luke 18:5. The unjust judge is driven to distraction by this widow's importunity. "At least let me do something to plead her case, so that she may not come anymore to torture me," he says. And then the Lord said, "You have heard what the judge of unrighteousness or injustice says."

Yes, the judge gave in, and he did what this woman wanted, but what was his motive? That he might not be bothered anymore. He was an unjust judge because he would do right only to get rid of someone who was a nuisance. What was the center of his life? Self—his quiet, his tranquillity. Let me not be disturbed. If doing what you want is going to give me peace, it doesn't matter whether it is right or wrong, I will do it.

Now, that is an injustice—doing things for other people simply because of one's personal benefit. We are to do things for others, not because of what rewards may accrue to us as a result, but because it is right.

You know, parents often act this way, and they do an injustice to their children. A little child comes to you and wants your attention. "Mom, do this for me, do that for me." And you just don't feel like it, or you don't have the time, or for some reason you just don't want to be bothered. Do you say, "Go look at television. I'm busy. Don't bother me."? That is an act of injustice toward your child. You are exposing him or her to all the dangers and the filth that exist on television just so they won't bother you.

Or some employee comes to you because there is something wrong, and he wants your time. The most convenient thing for you to do is just dismiss the case and say, "Forget it." Or you may give in just to get rid of that person. In either case, it is an act of injustice toward that person. Anything that is motivated by the desire to serve your best interests, in disregard of the other person, is an act of injustice. This is the man that we find here—the unjust judge.

The Core of All Sin and Injustice Is the Glorification of Self

And then I would like to call your attention to another passage of Scripture, John 7:18. Here we find our Lord in the temple teaching (see verse 14). All the people were admiring Him, saying, "Where did this man learn how to read and write? He never went to school; how can he teach us like

119

that?" (see verse 15). The Lord Jesus answered that His teaching was not His, but it came from the One who had sent Him, the Father. Now in verse 18 the Lord says, "He who speaks of himself seeks his own glory, but he who seeks the glory of him who sent him, he is true, *and there is no injustice in him.*" What does this mean? The Lord is saying, "I am not doing things for my own glory, but for the glory of the one who sent me, the Father. And if I am that way, there is no injustice in me." In other words, He would be unjust, He would not act properly toward others, if all He sought was His own glory.

The core, the center of injustice, is always self. The worst four letter word in the world today is not one that I cannot refer to on television or radio or print, but it is a word that is used constantly, SELF. The primary cause of divorce, the primary cause of injustice, the primary cause of failure toward our children, the primary cause of failure toward God, is SELF-glorification. May God deliver us from the glorification of self. May we not seek our own comfort at the expense of the suffering and needy of this world, and thus incur our Lord's condemnation, "Unjust!"

THINK IT OVER

1. What is the true evidence of salvation?
2. Why is it wrong to get people to profess to accept Christ without explaining that this entails full commitment of one's whole heart and life, in obedience to Him? (Jesus never accepted anything less in the Scriptures.)

3. Name three reasons the "unjust judge" was condemned by Christ.
4. Why are "sins of omission" as serious as sins of commission?
5. What is the core of all sin and injustice?

15

How Money Can Corrupt
Even A
Disciple of Christ

We have several instances in the New Testament in which a person or an action is called unjust. The next portion of Scripture that I would like to call to your attention in this regard is in Acts chapter 1 where we find Peter standing before 120 believers gathered in the upper room in Jerusalem. He is reviewing the arrest of the Lord Jesus Christ and the part played by Judas, who was the instrument of His betrayal.

How God Causes the Evil That Men Do to Further His Righteous Purposes

Especially note verse 17. Speaking of the prophecy of David concerning Judas, Peter says, "For he was counted to be among them [those who betrayed Jesus], and he received the portion of this ministry." Notice how this total thing is viewed by God as a ministry. In other words, the Lord Jesus came into this world to die. That was the way that He would redeem mankind. He was to be betrayed by someone, and that someone was Judas. The total thing is called a ministry, because it fulfilled the purposes of God. And as we view the sum total of evil in the world, we must grant the basic fact that God can accomplish His purposes even through the manifestations of the wrath of man. In this case, it was through an evil act perpetrated by Judas.

How very arresting this 17th verse is! It teaches us that though evil is not initiated by God, He can use it to fulfill His total purposes. If you don't look at it that way, you will go crazy. Look at your enemy, the one who betrays you, as part of the ministry that you are performing in the world. Did you ever think of that? Look at evil men and say they are part and parcel of God's total activity in the world. He is not responsible for their evil acts, but He uses them to further His own righteous purposes.

Judas Seduced by Unjust Gains

Peter goes on in verse 18 to say, "But he, Judas, bought or became the possesser of a field by means of the pay of unrighteousness or injustice"—by means of the remuneration that he received from an injustice that he perpetrated. The thirty pieces of silver that Judas received are called here the "pay of injustice." Significant, isn't it? Why are they called this? Judas, by betraying Jesus for thirty pieces of silver made possible the purchase by the high priests of a field to bury Jews who were foreign to Jerusalem and happened to die there (Matt. 27:3-10). In other words, this field was not purchased with money earned by honest labor but by Judas' act of unjust betrayal. That is unjust pay—payment that one receives for not working. I knew an otherwise honorable Christian woman who used to work periodically, and who wanted to take off from time to time also—and she found a very convenient way of doing it. She would work for six months and then quit, collect unemployment, and then go back to work and work the necessary time, and collect unemployment again. It became a cycle of life. I always thought that that was wrong.

Taking Pay for Work You Do Not Do Is Unjust

How many of us Christians fall into this trap? Is the money you use to buy something the result of your own work? Have you earned it or is it the pay of injustice? I am not talking of money received by inheritance, but of money obtained by taking unfair advantage of the law, or as the result of gambling, or defrauding others, or as payment for some questionable act or favor you have performed for others. Judas and the thirty pieces of silver he received are called "the pay of injustice." And I am afraid that in this world of ours, when we justify our laziness many times, when we just stand around and talk instead of working, do we realize we are defrauding our employer? We are not paid to talk, but to work. If you wanted to be a just person, and said to your employer at the end of the week, "Please deduct from my salary the hours I did not work during this time that I ought to have worked," how much money would you lose? Be honest, now. This is what the Word of God teaches me. There is a pay of injustice. Your boss may never discover your "goofing off," but remember that it is all written down in God's eternal record, and one day reviewing it will bring blushes to your face and mine, and there will be no coming back to do it over. Look at Judas. It was finished. He died and there was no undoing of his shame and act.

Money Can Blind the Eyes of Justice

Peter calls the thirty pieces of silver received by Judas "the wage," or as you have it in your English translation, "the

125

reward of iniquity." It is very interesting that every time that money is involved in our Lord's parables, there is iniquity or injustice—*adikia,* "unrighteousness"—involved.

We are actually still studying the 16th chapter of Luke, where we find the Parable of the Unjust Capitalist, the boss who would not pay his worker sufficient money and who fired him on hearsay. Now, he acted unjustly because money was involved.

In the case of Judas, he betrayed the Lord for thirty pieces of silver. Couldn't he have betrayed the Lord in some other way? He could simply have given the information of Jesus' whereabouts in Gethsemane, where He was praying for those who wanted to arrest Him.

Money Is Neutral: It Can Be Used for Good or Evil

But throughout the New Testament the Lord wants to tell us that money is simply a neutral commodity that can be used for either good or evil. He indicates that it is the best instrument to get you a welcoming committee in heaven, if you spend it rightly to win souls to Jesus Christ and to make friends for Him.

Money is like a knife. What would a cook do without a knife? And yet do you realize that most stabbing homicides occur in the kitchen between husband and wife? A knife is amoral. And, as they say today, "It isn't guns that kill people, it is people that kill people."

The Scriptures give us a comprehension of the true value of money. Money is very important, but it can be used for evil purposes. Here Judas betrayed the Lord for thirty pieces of silver. And Peter calls this "the wage of iniquity." Have you ever thought of how much that is? What would you take to betray Jesus?

126

Betrayal

Still as of old
Men by themselves are priced—
For thirty pieces Judas sold
Himself, not Christ.
—Hester H. Cholmondeley

For Judas in today's currency it took something like $10 to $20. To betray a person like the Lord Jesus Christ for that—was it worth it? No. Could it have been done another way? Yes, but in God's providence money was involved in the betrayal of the Lord Jesus Christ, so that He could show us what shameful things we can do sometimes for a little profit for self. Again it comes to the same thing: if you put self in the center, you will act unjustly toward others. If we could only learn this lesson I think we would be involved in the works of righteousness.

Now, the Lord could have pointed out Judas at the last supper, when He had told them that one of them would betray Him, and they had all begun to ask, "Is it I?" The easiest thing for the Lord to have done was to say to Judas "Yes, sir, it is you!" But He didn't do it. Why? Most likely He wanted to give Judas an opportunity at the last moment to repent. And this is how the grace of God works. He wants to give us an opportunity to the very last moment.

But observe what happened with the others when Jesus said one of them would betray Him. Immediately they began to question themselves. Did John have any reason to suspect that he could be the one to betray the Lord? No, he was in the closest circle, like Peter himself, and yet they were asking, "Is it I?"

Even Saints Need to Be on Guard Against Betraying the Lord by Unworthy Actions

One of the greatest lessons we can learn in life is to be on our guard against a betrayal of the Lord. You may be the best worker in the world, the best saint in your community, but never lose sight of the possibility that you may be betraying the Lord Jesus Christ by doing less than your best, and in a moment of weakness may fall as low as Peter in his moment of denial. When the Lord says, "Watch out for that pay of iniquity, of injustice," is it possible He means me? Yes, it is possible, and he who is on guard will never fall; but he who thinks that there is no one more godly than himself, and that he is absolutely impervious to the temptations to betray his Lord for advantage, is the one who needs to watch all the more carefully. "Pride goeth before destruction," remember, "and an haughty spirit before a fall" (Prov. 16:18).

Are You Guilty of Doing "A Favor of Injustice"?

One further lesson we must learn from Judas's act of betrayal is that it is an unjust act to receive pay to do an innocent man or woman harm. Judas bargained with the Pharisees what sum of money they would accept for him to betray the Lord Jesus (Matt. 26:16). That is "pay of injustice," and we must be very careful, because sometimes it is possible that we act like that indirectly. We feel that we can curry favor with someone by believing a rumor he is spreading about another person. If we accept this without further proof, because we know that somehow it is going to bring us into a good relationship with that person who says it, either now or in the future, that is "a favor of injustice." In other words, we must not allow ourselves to benefit personally—whether the benefit is money or a closer relationship with that person—by selling out the reputation of an innocent person. For instance, if I accept an accusation against one of my brethren, and do not challenge that accusation because I want to be favored by the accuser, any benefit I derive from my cowardice is the same as the pay of injustice that Judas received.

The Lord Jesus was an innocent person. Didn't Judas know it? How much longer did he need to live with the Lord Jesus in order to know that it was an innocent man whom he was betraying? He was absolutely sure of Jesus' innocence, as he confessed when he flung the money back at the feet of the chief priests and elders (see Matt. 27:4, 5). And I believe that because of the certainty of the innocence of Jesus, that made those thirty pieces of silver that much more "the pay of injustice."

THINK IT OVER

1. Give one or more instances in Scripture in which men's evil deeds were used to further God's purposes for good. (See Gen. 50:16-21; Daniel 3:16ff.; chapter 4 also.)

2. How can money be a lure to sin even for Christians? Name as many ways as you can think of (such as compromising with dishonest practices for fear of losing one's job, etc.).

3. Correct this often misquoted statement by looking up the exact words of Scripture: "Money is the root of all evil." (See I Timothy 6:10.)

16

A Man Who
Sought to Buy the Gift
of God With Money

Now, we have another incident in the 8th chapter of the Acts of the Apostles that concerned a man by the name of Simon in Samaria. In verse 23 we find an interesting expression: "Because I see thee, that you are in the gall of bitterness, and the bond of injustice, or the conspiracy of injustice." The King James version translates it as "the bond of iniquity." Go back to verse 9 to begin the story about this man Simon, and then we shall undertake to analyze it.

"But there was a certain man, called Simon, which beforetime in the same city used sorcery, and bewitched the people of Samaria, giving out that himself was some great one: to whom they all gave heed, from the least to the greatest, saying, This man is the great power of God."

Be cautious; all individuals who become famous and are acclaimed as doing great things for God are not necessarily genuine. "And to him they had regard, because that of long time he had bewitched them with sorceries. But when they believed Philip [who was the evangelist in Samaria] preaching the things concerning the kingdom of God, and the name of Jesus Christ, they were baptized, both men and women. Then Simon himself believed also: and when he was baptized, he continued with Philip, and wondered, beholding the miracles and signs which were done. Now when the apostles which were at Jerusalem heard that Samaria had received the word of God, they sent unto them Peter and John [two apostles]: who, when they were come down, prayed for them, that they might receive the Holy Ghost: (for as yet he was fallen upon none of them: only they were baptized in the name of the Lord Jesus.) Then laid they their hands on them, and they received the Holy Ghost. And when Simon saw that through laying on of the apostles' hands the Holy Ghost was given, he offered them money [Observe once again, that money is involved in injustice.], saying, Give me also this power, that on whomsoever I lay hands, he may receive the Holy Ghost."

Money, the Holy Spirit, injustice, are all mixed up in this one incident. "But Peter said unto him, Thy money perish with thee, because thou hast thought that the gift of God may be purchased with money. Thou has neither part nor lot in this matter: for thy heart is not right in the sight of God. Repent therefore of this thy wickedness, and pray God, if perhaps the thought of thine heart may be forgiven thee. For I perceive that thou art in the gall of bitterness [Who? A man who was performing miracles], and in the bond of iniquity." There you have the conspiracy of injustice.

What does it mean to be "a conspirator of injustice"—the accusation that Peter leveled against Simon the sorcerer in Samaria? Just so that you may have an idea, let me review the Biblical background. Philip was one of the seven elected by the apostles in Jerusalem to serve at tables. This did not mean, of course, that they were limited to manual work.

Fortunately unions were not in existence at that time to tell people that they had to do one specific task, and never touch anything else that needed to be done. It is good to be a specialist, but it is not good to be a slave of your specialty. Philip felt that he should not only minister at the tables in Jerusalem, but that he should also do the work of an evangelist. Nothing hindered him from doing that. He received no apostolic rebuke when he decided to do this. And he was not alone of the seven in preaching the Word of God, for Stephen did this also, who was stoned and became the first martyr of the Christian Church.

So Philip came to Samaria, which is next to Judah, not very far from Jerusalem, approximately an hour or so by car today. And the Lord attended his ministry with great blessing. In Samaria he met a man by the name of Simon, who was a magician, a sorcerer who was able to attract the crowds, which acclaimed him as the power of God.

And later on we find that Peter calls him a man "in the gall of bitterness, and in a conspiracy or a bond of injustice" (Acts 8:23). There are several reasons why Peter calls him that. Nobody else in the Scriptures has been described in these harsh terms, that from him there emanated a bitter attitude and bitter words, and that he was a conspirator with injustice.

Now, why? First, because this man was acclaimed as a power in the hands of God when in reality he was a fraud. He was deceiving others to think of how great he was, while he knew that in reality he was not related in any sense to God, though he was proclaimed a healer, a man who worked miracles. And only against such a man are such words spoken by an apostle.

Be Careful of Modern-Day "Simons"

I am afraid that we have many Simons in our day who

133

make everybody believe that through the power of God they perform miracles, when in reality they are nothing but frauds, deceivers, even as Simon. Let us not be deceived ourselves in judging miracles and extraordinary demonstrations as being necessarily the power of God. We should be extremely careful.

This man Simon was baptized by none other than Philip himself. See how easy it is to be deceived? And yet he was a fraud, an unjust man, who tried to make the people believe that he had the power of God.

Secondly, this man was wealthy. He thought that his money could buy anything, even the power of the Holy Spirit. Did you observe, he did not *ask,* but *demanded* this power in exchange for money? There were two groups in Samaria; the first group was the common people who had observed Simon, and then had seen Philip work miracles, true miracles, through the power of God. They became attracted to Philip, recognizing what he did as reality, as genuine, and they believed and were baptized. The second group was composed of Philip, followed by Peter and John, who came to Samaria from Jerusalem to see what was going on. And we find out in this passage of Scripture that most of the common people had left Simon and believed the Gospel that Philip was preaching. They were baptized of course, by Philip, and apparently the apostles confirmed their baptism as being genuine because they evidenced genuine faith. But Simon also had believed in Philip (and not necessarily in Jesus Christ as His Savior and Lord), and he also was baptized, but his faith and baptism were not confirmed by Peter and John, the apostles. Instead he was condemned as a conspirator of injustice, as a man full of gall.

Why? Because it became evident how false his faith and baptism were when he saw that the Holy Spirit was coming upon these people confirming their belief, and he wanted to buy the power to perform this miracle. He thought he could buy the power of the Holy Spirit with money.

Discerning Whether the Spirit of God Is at Work in "Miracle-Workers" Today

You see again an instance of injustice related to the use of money. And where did he get all this money? By performing sorceries and miracles. He was a rich man, like many "Simons" who live in our day. Who are the preachers who are rolling in wealth? The frauds, those people who say, "Come to me, and I will heal your many diseases," yet most of the wheelchair victims go out as they came in. Cures? Yes—but mainly psychological, and seldom able to be documented. I have wondered many times whether the Spirit of God is really upon them or not.

Peter comes and puts this man in his place. With his apostolic discernment and perception he confirmed the others, but this man, Simon the sorcerer, he condemned, in spite of the fact that he claimed to have believed, was baptized, and was a great miracle worker. He was a deceiver.

I believe that many times we do not have the ability to discern who is a true believer and who is not. If Philip could be deceived, so can you and I. Especially be wary, any time when money is involved in offering something that God gives as a gift. Look at verse 20, "And Peter said unto him, Your silver, let it be unto you and unto your perditional loss, because the gift of God you thought you were going to obtain with money." He who mixes up the free gift of God and his own money is a conspirator. Study this passage carefully and arrive at your own conclusions.

135

THINK IT OVER

1. Did Jesus Christ ever ask or receive money for healing anyone?
2. How did Simon the sorcerer make his money before he professed to be a Christian?
3. Why do you think he wanted the ability to bestow the Holy Spirit on new believers?
   a. To be a blessing to them spiritually?
   b. To enhance his own reputation as a miracle worker?
   c. To turn it to his monetary profit?
4. What is one of the marks of a present-day "Simon"?

17

Life's Little Gifts Entail
Great Responsibilities

Let's consider more thoughtfully all that is implied in our Lord's axiomatic statement in Luke 16:10, as He concluded the parable of the unjust rich man, and his dealings with his steward. These words of our Lord ought to be kept before our mind's eye in capital letters all the time. They will change our outlook on life, enhance our chances of promotion, and enable us to achieve things that would otherwise be impossible.

The lessons in our Lord's parables are extremely important for our daily lives. In Luke 16:10 He said, "He who is faithful in that which is least is faithful also in much." Actually there is no verb in the Greek text: "He who in little faithful is faithful in much." The word *pistos,* "faithful," used here, actually has the meaning of "dependable." He who is dependable in the least little thing that most people would ordinarily not pay any attention to is the type of person who will be dependable in great things.

Do You Always Return the Right Change?

When I was a little fellow of six or seven, it seems that I was a financier from the beginning. At that time I was living in Khartoum, Sudan. A kind man named Stelios Costantinides (who is a good friend of our work now) used to test me in a very interesting way. I will never forget it, for it made a man of me. He would give me sufficient money and a little over to buy something, and then wait to see whether I would return the change. If you don't think this is a good test of character, try it on your own youngsters. The temptation is very great, the change is very little, and who will know the difference if you don't return all of it? He never asked how much the soda or ice cream cone cost—just how much I had spent. I had to be truthful, so I took the money out and gave him the right change. Well, that was tremendous training for me.

The Lord will not usually entrust you all at once with a great responsibility. He has more understanding of "what is in man" than that. Check up on yourself, and if you have not been entrusted with much, perhaps you have not proven faithful in little things. What do you do with a small opportunity? It is possible to hide from our parents, our supervisors, and most other people what we do with our time, money, and talents; but we may be sure that God knows everything down to the smallest detail. And what the Lord is saying here is, don't despise small opportunities. Show your character by doing well and faithfully the little duties of life.

A Lesson From a Pair of Shoes

Our family was very poor when I was a child, and my mother had to work hard so that I could go to school. I remember that every year, in grade school and high school, some philanthropists in the Greek schools I was attending in Cairo, Egypt, distributed shoes to needy children, and I was among them. That's one of the reasons why when I came to the United States, I became involved in relieving the sufferings of others. One of the first things I initiated was sending Bundles of Love to destitute children at Christmas, each of which contained a pair of shoes.

My mother always watched to see what care I would take of this pair of shoes that came to me free of charge. That's one way a person's character is known—how he deals with something that he didn't have to pay for. I'll never forget how pleased my mother was every day as she watched me polish those shoes. I took such good care of them that they lasted me a whole year. When I saw them wearing out, I would cut pieces of rubber from old tires and glue them underneath and stuff the shoes with newspapers. I knew they must last me for the whole year, because there would be no other shoes until Christmas came around again. And my mother said to me, "My boy, you'll make something of yourself someday, because you've taken care of a pair of shoes that has been given to you."

Now, you may think that's silly, but it's not; it's the beginning of true stewardship. It is not how you would spend a million dollars if you had it, but how you spend the one dollar you do have that shows what you are. It is not how you use the opportunities and privileges you wish you had, but it is how you use the least opportunity, the least amount of money, and the least privilege that is given to you.

Every one of us thinks that what he has is too little. Even a millionaire thinks he is less favorably situated than a multi-millionaire. But if you value that which you have and use it dependably, I guarantee that both God and others will entrust you with far greater privileges and opportunities. If you fail to acquire the sense of dependability in "little things," those who live around you will drop you like a hotcake when they have an important job they want done, even as God will drop you because He cannot trust you with anything. Prove yourself dependable and you will find yourself accomplishing greater things than you thought possible. Don't say the world is cruel because you don't receive a new pair of shoes every two or three months. Say "What a wonderful privilege it is to have one pair of shoes; I will take care of them. And when people see how I care for them, they will trust me; and I'll be given a good job and earn enough money to buy my own shoes." But watch out! When you earn enough, you may be in danger of losing your sense of dependability. This is the lesson, a very important one, that our Lord is teaching us here.

May God give us a sense of value for the little gifts of life, and help us to realize that He will entrust us—and others will entrust us—with much more if we prove faithful and dependable in "that which is least."

THINK IT OVER

1. How dependable are you in the following "little things" in your job?
   a. Getting to work on time? _____
   b. Giving a full hour's work for each hour's pay?_____
   c. Not helping yourself to even a postage stamp without paying for it? _____
2. Are you as dependable in keeping promises to a child as you are to an adult? _____
3. Do you remember to pay back even a small loan you have made from someone in a moment of need? _____
4. Do you do such a menial task as cleaning your room "as unto the Lord"—without skimping the corners? _____

140

18

It Takes a Great God to be Concerned With Little Things

Think of all the insects God has created, and reflect on the fact that He has created every one of them with the same perfection as He created the entire universe. When our Lord was here on earth, He talked about how God pays attention to and cares for the things that seem to be most insignificant as far as man is concerned.

God Cares About the Sparrows, the Lilies, and the Very Hairs of Our Head

For instance, in Matthew 10:29 He said, "Are not two sparrows sold for a farthing?" That was about half a penny—next to nothing. A sparrow is one of the most insignificant of birds; men attribute little value to it; but how does God look upon it? Jesus says, "And one of them shall not fall on the ground without your Father." In other words, He cares for the sparrows; He pays attention to what most people esteem of little value. No matter how small we may seem in our own estimation or in the eyes of others, our Lord assures us, "Ye are of more value than many sparrows" (v. 31).

Again in the Sermon on the Mount, in Matthew 6:28, 29, our Lord said, "Consider the lilies of the field, how they grow; they toil not, neither do they spin: and yet I say unto you, That even Solomon in all his glory was not arrayed like one of these." In other words, "I have put more attention on a lily than man has put on Solomon's most glorious attire. I pay attention to the smallest things, for I know that these make up the sum total of life."

When Jesus said, "But the very hairs of your head are all numbered," He was reminding us of the attention that God has paid in the creation, maintenance, and sustenance of the smallest things of life. We ought to marvel at them also. God is never lost in the vastness of the magnificent. He condescends to infinite details, and He builds a new universe in the smallest thing. That is just as perfect, and He gives it as careful attention as He has given to the entire universe.

To Pay Attention to "That Which Is Least" Is Godlike

How can we be like Him in this? I read about a writer who said he treated every letter that he wrote as if it were a book that would make the bestseller list. Pay attention to the small things; they make the difference. They affect the lives of others, and they affect your own life, as they reflect your character. They are what other people judge you by.

God's watchfulness over little things is a trait we should seek to imitate in our daily lives. He does not cease to be God by giving attention to the smallest diatom in the bottom of the sea. One of our greatest dangers is to consider ourselves so big we have no time to give to details. When we can't be bothered about a little thing that may affect the lives of others, or our very own, we show how small we are. Our great God paid as much attention to designing the aerodynamics of the bumblebee as He did to the whole universe and its laws. We show how small we are when we fail to appreciate how important little things are. This applies to the letters that we write, the conversations we have with the least important persons, and even to our dealings with little children in fairness and courtesy. Such things show our character far more accurately than how we treat our superiors. The manner in which we treat the last person that anyone would pay attention to reveals whether we are Godlike or not.

THINK IT OVER

1. Do you ever worry that, with all the "important" people and events God has to look after in this world, He may not pay much attention to you?

2. List as many Scripture verses as you can that reassure you of God's personal concern for you. (Here are 3 to get you started: Matthew 10:29; I Peter 5:7; Philippians 4:19.)

3. Do you show loving concern for the seemingly unimportant people you know or meet?

19

The Humility of Christ in Identifying Himself With the Poor and Lowly

Now let us look at our Lord to see how faithful and dependable He was in little things. One thing that stands out above all others is that He paid attention to people and things that others did not think much of. He did not consider it beneath the dignity of God's Son to be born in a manger. He identified Himself with the poor and neglected, with those who needed Him most, instead of with the rich and influential.

The Lord Never Abused His Power in Dealing With Others

The Lord never took advantage of others. Though He asked them to follow Him, to give all that they had, it was not for His own comfort and benefit, but for the extension of God's Kingdom through the spread of the Gospel.

There was a king whose officers, in the midst of battle, decided to go and take food that was desperately needed from some homes in the area. When they came back with it, the king asked, "Did you pay them for what you took?"

They said, "No, the king doesn't pay."

He said, "Go back and pay them for everything that you took away."

A king who arbitrarily takes things away from people is hated, but a ruler who pays for everything he needs, and that people are willing to give up, is the one who is loved. Anyone who uses his power to take away, is abusing his power. He who uses his power to protect the little fellow, rather than taking away his possessions thinking they belong to him because of his superior position, is a great person. The way we deal with people who are below us socially or in accomplishment or possessions shows how great or how small we are. The Lord Jesus Christ proved that He was God by stooping to the smallest things, and the lowliest persons, contrary to ordinary human nature. Man that is not redeemed by Jesus Christ tends to be a showoff, a grabber. He looks down upon others.

From the time He was born in a stable, our Lord lived the life of a common laborer for most of His years on earth. And during the three years of His preaching and miracle-working ministry, He never lived above the poverty level. "He had not where to lay his head." He could have established a commuting service, don't you think, between heaven and earth? Then every time He came down, He would be greatly admired. "Oh, look, here's the only person who can prove while He's on earth that He's the Son of Man; and while He's in heaven, He's the Son of God."

I wonder how we would have used our power if we were in His place. Instead He chose the most secluded places, the poorest homes to go to. Just once He chose the home of a rich man when He visited the home of Zacchaeus in Jericho. All the other homes He chose to go to were humble dwellings, such as the home of Martha, Mary, and Lazarus in

Bethany. He entered the home of Zacchaeus only because He knew His presence was needed there to bring conviction to this man.

He went about doing good every day in the most quiet manner and the most secluded places. He was transfigured only once to show His deity to three of His disciples. He could have been transfigured many times before the multitudes, but the Lord Jesus was not a show-off. If His words and deeds did not bring conviction, He knew putting on a big display would only influence people for the wrong reasons. When He was being tried by Pilate, He could have struck him dead in an instant, but He didn't do it. It is the sign of a great person not to be in a hurry to show His greatness, but to wait for God's time.

Power Can Be Good or Bad, Christlike or Corrupt

How do we deal with little people? How do we deal with the power that we possess? "He that is faithful in that which is least is faithful also in much." Power can be Godlike or it can be manlike. Take healings, for instance. The Lord did not establish an inherent ability in people, even in Christians, to be healers. He gave gifts of healings to be exercised at the proper times to accomplish His purposes. But He has not given inherent power for any human being to heal at will, because power corrupts and does not treat small things and small people in a Godlike manner.

God grant that we may learn from our Lord the restraint of power, the gentleness of serving instead of being served. Grant that we may never abuse others who are under us. They are there not to be commanded but to be protected and to be lifted up. May we be Christlike in our attitude in dealing with small things and seemingly unimportant people.

Our Lord gave us a principle that, if followed, would

revolutionize each of our lives. It could revolutionize every community and nation. He commended dependability in small things.

Great people are not necessarily those who attempt to do great things. They are the men and women who have the character to accomplish great things. And they have proven that character in the way they have handled little things. Our Savior provided not only a word of admiration, not only the prescription for such behavior, but He also provided the example.

I was just thinking, if there were a person who could walk on the sea like Him, would he do it just once in an emergency to rescue some men in a foundering boat, or would he do it every time he wanted to cross over, instead of taking a little boat as was Jesus' usual custom? Jesus did it once and that was enough. Give me another man in history who could walk on the sea who would do it only once. Jesus would rather have the company of His disciples in a boat and go to sleep while they were struggling to go across, than demonstrate how great He was on a constant basis.

The really great person is not one who constantly shows off his superior powers over others, but one who struggles along with them when He could have avoided the difficulty with the greatest of ease. That is our Savior. Study His life and you will understand true greatness. He who shows off every time that he is able to is not Godlike. The truly Godlike person is one who knows when to show how great he is and when to restrain his greatness. Jesus could have stilled the sea of Galilee every time it became turbulent and life-threatening, but He didn't do it. He is selective. I believe the reason God did not give inherent power to any man always to do great and mighty things was that he would become intolerable. To be superior, and not to show it every time you talk to someone, takes divine restraint. If you constantly flaunt your superior knowledge or ability, you will become obnoxious. Ability must be restrained by wisdom.

And again I say that there is a reason why, in the gifts of the Holy Spirit enumerated by Paul in the 12th chapter of I Corinthians, the first gift of the Spirit is not miraculous powers, such as gifts of healings, but it is the word of wisdom. Our Lord warns us to watch out, lest pride be our motivation for aiming at high things, while we overlook the daily tasks that fall to our lot.

A Great Sculptor Who Took Infinite Pains With Small Details

Probably no greater sculptor ever lived than Michelangelo. One day after he had spent a great deal of time on a statue, a critic said, "Why, you haven't accomplished anything in all this time!"

"Oh," he said, "Haven't I? I have worked for months on how to refine the lips of this character, to portray the muscles."

And the other fellow said, "That isn't important."

"Oh," he responded, "I attribute great importance to the little things." And Michelangelo is remembered because he cared how the lips of a person on a statue appeared, how the muscles gave them the right expression, in spite of the fact that he had to spend a great deal of time on it.

Would to God that every child was raised to respect this plain, basic principle taught by our Savior, of dependability in little things, whether it be in washing dishes or handling his finances. Character is revealed in little things. Observe how people handle them and you will know the great people from the small people.

How we need to pray for grace to be like our Savior—to

149

pay attention to the little things of life, not to show off and try to attempt great things every time we're able to, but to keep company with people of like human frailties as ourselves, in a spirit of helpfulness and humility.

THINK IT OVER

1. If you are in a position of authority, are you unreasonably demanding and bossy, or firm but courteous?

2. Do you always demand that others serve you, or are you willing to serve others in a Christlike spirit of helpfulness and caring?

3. Do you secretly enjoy showing off your superiority when with others, "hogging the show," as it were, or are you content to let others express their viewpoints without always feeling the need of putting them down?

4. Are you sensitive to the feelings of others, so that you refrain from sarcasm and unnecessary criticism in dealing with those who have not had your educational or social advantages? (See Romans 12:16.)

20

Further Insights Into Our Lord's Dealings With Small People and Little Things

Let us look a little further at the life of our Lord to see how He behaved toward small people and little things. The 9th chapter of the Gospel of John gives us the story of His meeting with a blind beggar outside the temple. The disciples immediately wanted to know who was responsible for this man's condition. Was it his own sin or that of his parents? The Lord said it was neither of these, but for the glory of God, and He healed him. He told him to go wash in the Pool of Siloam, and he saw.

You would think that the Lord would then dismiss this man from His mind. After all, he was only a blind beggar. But amazingly enough, in the 35th verse of this chapter we find that He went looking for him again to converse with him. What great man would do a thing like that? Yet our Lord's greatness consisted not only in giving sight to a blind beggar, but in the respect that He gave him by seeking him out to talk with him. It impressed me a great deal as an example of paying attention to little things, small people.

Dying in Agony, He Provides for His Mother

Or take an incident connected with our Lord's crucifixion. In the hour of His greatest agony, immediately preceding His death, what does He do? He gives thought to His mother. He says to her, referring to John, "Here's your son," and to John He says, "Here is your mother." He didn't forget His mother. You know, the greatest person is the one who at the height of his glory remembers the duty he owes to others. The cross wasn't the height of Christ's agony; it wasn't the height of His suffering; it was the height of God's glory manifest in the flesh. And in that greatest moment of agony and glory He remembered His earthly mother. "Father, into thy hands I commend my spirit," but before He did that He took thought for His mother.

He Carefully Folded the Napkin—Why?

Well, let's go to His tomb. You remember the detail of the napkin with which His head was wrapped being found there in perfect order? It wasn't disturbed at all. Why is this recorded? What does such a little detail have to do with the resurrection story? It tells us that the One who raised Himself from the dead wasn't in any hurry. He didn't rush to escape, but He calmly took the napkin off His head and folded it up and laid it down in perfect order. A little thing with great meaning.

Little Things That Reveal Character

Whenever I visit a private home—and I visit many in my travels around the world, I make it a practice always to make my bed after arising. One time a travelling companion made fun of me. He said, "You don't have to make your bed." I didn't have to, but making my bed seemed to me an indication of Christian thoughtfulness. And may the Lord forgive me, but I've never had much respect for the person who doesn't. The little things of life make up a large part of our character.

I remember at one time I received an invitation from a young preacher to speak in his church. He said, "I remember when you preached at my father's church many years ago. And my mother had worked all night, and after dinner, you did the dishes. I'll never forget that. I forgot your sermon, but I haven't forgotten your doing dishes at my mother's home."

A little thing? You may laugh at it, but you will never know how far-reaching the results may be if you pay attention to the little things of life.

"Peter, Put Your Shoes On!"

And one more incident comes to mind. You remember the account in Acts 12 of how Peter was taken prisoner in Jerusalem, and an angel came to liberate him. I can just imagine impulsive Peter saying, "Let's get out of here." And the angel saying in effect, "Wait a minute. Put your shoes on. Take your time. Put your coat on. Take your time. Don't be in such a hurry, be orderly." And if you're orderly in the little things, you'll be orderly in great things. He who is dependable in small things will be entrusted with greater responsibilities. Let's follow our Lord's example.

Trifles

The massive gates of circumstance
Are turned upon the smallest hinge,
And what oft seems some petty chance
Gives to our life its after tinge.
The trifles of our daily lives
The little things scarce worth recall,

Of which no visible trace survives,
They are the mainsprings after all.
                              —Author Unknown

THINK IT OVER

1. What does it tell you about a person's character if he
   a. Throws his coat across a chair?
   b. Drapes his tie over a bedpost?
   c. Drops his wet towels on the bathroom floor?
2. What does it tell about a person's character who
   a. Puts the cap back on the toothpaste?
   b. Helps clean up after a church supper?
   c. Thanks people sincerely for whatever small or large act of kindness they do for him or for his organization or church?

21

The Rewards
of Being Faithful in
"That Which Is Least"

What are the rewards of being faithful in the small things of life? First of all, unless you prove yourself in something small, you will not be given an opportunity to try something big. Most people who assign responsibilities have a sense of responsibility themselves, and will not assign great responsibilities to people who have not proven themselves in the smaller things with which they have been entrusted.

The First Two Rewards—a Wider Sphere of Service and Greater Expertise

The reward of fidelity in small things, then, is that it prepares us for, and opens the way to a wider sphere of service. The question each of us must ask is, am I missing the opportunity to do something greater in life because I have not proven myself in the little responsibilities that are mine day by day?

Another reward is that I can do my next task better because of serious, previous efforts. Perfection is not achieved automatically. If every task that I do gives me a greater expertise, then I'll be able to do my work much faster and better each time I attempt it. So it is to my advantage to acquire that expertise by doing my work in the best way possible. It makes me more proficient.

For instance, in preparing a sermon, if I put my best effort into it, striving each time to improve the content of a message through diligence in prayer and study of the Word of God, then I will preach better and better sermons. But if I just turn my "sermon barrel" upside down and dig out something I have preached in the past, I'll be a mediocre preacher. It is a great temptation for a preacher to use what he has given in the past, adding nothing to it. It can save him much study and work.

The Temptation to Do Less Than Our Best

We are all subject to the temptation to do less than our best at times. Every temptation resisted weakens the force of all other temptations. For instance, the temptation to steal a large sum of money seldom comes all at once. It comes little by little. "Oh, who cares about a dollar; it's nothing; he won't miss it." Have you ever heard anything like that? He may not miss it, but it weakens your resistance to a greater temptation that may come along your way later on. Victory over temptation lies with the person who recognizes his weaknesses and prepares to meet the attack of the enemy. Resisting the temptations that come along your way day by day is very important; otherwise you may find that yielding to sin has become a way of life with you.

If we yield to the temptation to become used to doing less than our best, to do only as much as everybody else does, we will deprive the other persons with whom we associate— whether wife, husband, child, boss, or whoever—of the best that is in us.

156

For instance, what is our attitude when we hear God's name taken in vain in a conversation by others? Do we dare to show our disapproval, or are we afraid to speak up? If we do not resist the first time, then later on we won't have the courage to resist an open attack upon the faith we hold so precious. Every time we fail to resist a small temptation, we weaken our ability to resist a greater one. And every time we resist a temptation, it becomes easier to resist a greater temptation. Small things hold great potential for good or evil. Small things done well increase our possibility of doing greater things.

THINK IT OVER

1. In preparing a sermon or Sunday school lesson does it really matter whether you look up the exact wording of Scripture, or simply try to slide by on your memory?

2. In preparing a book report are you being fair to the author in passing judgment simply by skimming through a few paragraphs here and there?

3. In handling money—whether in business or for the church—are you scrupulous to account for every penny—or does a dollar or more find its way into your own pocket now and then?

4. Is your recipe for success:
   a. "Do only as much as is needed to get by"—
   b. Or "Whatsoever ye do, do it heartily, as to the Lord, and not unto men" (Col. 3:23)?

22

Three Important Contrasts to Help Us Live in the Light of Eternal Values

At the conclusion of the parable about the rich man and his dismissed business manager, our Lord gave us some very important statements concerning life itself. You remember that the basic principle of this parable was that we as Christians should use our lives of faith in a way that would count the most for eternity.

The First Contrast—Between the "Least" and the "Much"

In Luke 16:10, 11, and 12 we are given three instructive contrasts. Verse 10 speaks of "He that is faithful in that which is least. [In Greek, "the faithful or the dependable one in the least"]." There our Lord tells us there is something that is least in this life; it has the lowest value. And He concludes the verse by saying, "is also faithful [or dependable] in much." The contrast here is between "least" and "much." Many things in this life that we value greatly are really the least important. And there are things which we will greatly value in eternity

159

which in this life we seem to value very little. We do not always evaluate things properly. What is of little value and what is of much value—that is the first contrast.

The Second Contrast—Between the Unrighteous Mammon and That Which Is of Real Value

And then in verse 11 we see that there is a second contrast: "If therefore ye have not been faithful in the unrighteous mammon . . . ." Now, right where you are, you are challenged about your faithful use of money, the unrighteous mammon. Mammon is the god of material things, of money. He is unrighteous. The Greek word is *adikos*. What it means is that he causes people to be selfish. When you have material things and you use them selfishly, you use them in unjust, unrighteous ways. And Christ finishes the verse by saying, "who will entrust you with the true riches?" There's the contrast: the unrighteous mammon and that which is of real value.

The Third Contrast—Between What Belongs to Somebody Else That You Are Responsible for, and What Is Really Yours

In verse 12 we have the third contrast: "And if in that which is another's." There haven't been too many sermons preached on this particular text. "And if ye have not been faithful in that which is another's, who shall give you that which is your own?" The contrast is between that which is somebody else's that you have the responsibility of investing or caring for, and that which is really yours.

In these three verses we have one main contrast which is the material and the spiritual. First of all, any material thing is really, when you come down to it, of little value. Any spiritual thing is really of great value. Second, material things tend to

160

make the owner unrighteous, selfish. Isn't that true? A person who has ten dollars can be just as selfish as the person who has a million. It all depends on the attitude.

But the least spiritual value makes you really richer than the person who has an abundance of material goods. And whether you possess material things in small or great amounts, are they really yours? What the Lord is saying in effect here is, "They're really not yours; they're somebody else's. You're just holding them." God grant we may not be buried like that rich king who was laid in his casket with his hands clenched, because the people wanted to show that what he took, he'd never let go. In the final analysis, when you close your eyes in death, others find that what you thought was yours, and which you didn't realize was really not yours, is now theirs. So the Lord tells us, "One of the greatest things you need to realize is that what you have, any material thing, is not really yours, it is somebody else's. But that which is of a spiritual nature can change your character, and that is always yours in this life and in eternity."

Three contrasts, and we are going to dwell upon them because they are so important for us to understand. May God help us to realize how little value material things have, and that they tend to make us selfish. May we also realize that they are not really ours, while spiritual realities are indeed great because they are life changing; they *thus outlast us,* so that they are really ours for time and in eternity. An unknown poet expressed this truth in these lines:

Ben Adam had a golden coin one day,
　　Which he put out at current interest due.
Year after year awaiting him it lay,
　　Until the double coin two pieces grew,
And these two four—and so on, till people said,
　　"How rich Ben Adam is!" and bowed the servile head.

161

Ben Selim had a golden coin that day,
   Which to a stranger asking alms he gave,
Who went rejoicing on his unknown way.
   But Selim died, too poor to own a grave;
But when his soul reached heaven, angels with pride
   Showed him the wealth to which his coin had multiplied.

THINK IT OVER

1. Three simple tests to determine whether you value material or spiritual things most:
   a. Do you tithe the interest on your bank accounts? (In fact, do you tithe at all?)
   b. If a guest breaks something of value in your home, do you mourn more for your broken possession, or for your guest's consternation, embarrassment, and dismay? That is, would you say, "Oh, my beautiful vase!" or "Don't feel badly; accidents will happen; I've caused them myself, so let's not be upset about it"?
   c. If God called you to serve Him at less money than you could make in the business world, what would your reaction be?

23

The First Contrast:
The "Least" and the "Much"

When our Lord brings into contrast the material things of life with the spiritual, He calls the one "the least" and the other "the much." What He means by this is that we should give them their relative values. Man tends to go to extremes. Some people will sit on the beach and brown their bodies in the sun for five hours or more, but will not take five minutes to pray, or to study the Word of God, or to read a book that concerns their spiritual welfare.

Achieving a Proper Set of Values in Life

On what do you place the greatest value? Do you look at something of little value as though through a great microscope and see it so enlarged that it deceives you into giving it far more importance, time, and effort than it is worth?

Our Lord is saying here, "Be careful about the importance you ascribe to the things that really should be considered the least in this life. The value that you place on them determines your estimate of the spiritual things of life that are so much more important." After all, it is the soul that survives the body, and yet how much of our time is taken up with concern for our body and how much for our soul? Just think of how much greater your spiritual stature would be if you spent half the time some people spend looking into the mirror, looking rather into the mirror of the Word of God to reveal your soul blemishes instead of the wrinkles on your face.

Our Lord Recognized Material Things Are Needful for Life

Now, we must realize that our Savior did not say material things are nothing and the spiritual is everything. The person who says that is not a realist, but man's depraved nature is polarized. It goes either to one extreme or the other. What is needed is a sense of proportion.

I believe that one of the most significant words in the New Testament is *tassoo,* which means "to place in its proper category." For instance, in connection with the word "subject," *hupotassoo,* which means "to place in a category under you," we need to avoid going to extremes in its application. The Apostle Paul admonishes men in their attitude toward women to let them be subject to their husbands. And what does "super-Christian" do? He says, "Oh, that indicates my superiority. That's my authority to rule over my wife. She'd better do what I say or else." Such reasoning is so confused it isn't even funny. All that the Apostle Paul is saying is, "Woman, recognize who you are, and the category in which you belong. You must know who you are and who your husband is. He is over you, not to kick you around but to protect you. Husbands, place your wives under you, but not so low as your feet to kick them, but only as low as your hearts to love them and protect them with your arms around them."

164

Recognition of Different Categories of Persons and Things Essential to Proper Evaluation

Each person and object in life must be evaluated in its own category. Material things are absolutely necessary. You cannot live without them. But do you give proper importance to spiritual values? How much do you spend on entertainment for the body? How much do you spend for the growth and the satisfaction of your spiritual hungers? Don't confuse values. This is what our Lord is saying. Look at that which is of little value and give it its proper place. If necessary, give it up for that which is of much value. Otherwise you will be an unbalanced person and will suffer for it. May God give us discernment in giving proper value to those things that are necessary for life.

THINK IT OVER

1. Can you give a clear statement of your own set of values in life? For instance, which is more important to you: "Keeping up with the Joneses" or a life style that enables you to give generously to the Lord's work?
2. Rate these in order of importance in your life from 1—6. (Neither should be exclusive of another—but which is more important?)
   a. Your monthly income   _____
   b. Your eternal salvation   _____
   c. Being on friendly terms with the people you meet

      _____
   d. Standing up for what is right, whether it's popular or not   _____
   e. Your daily newspapers   _____
   f. Studying God's Word   _____

24

The Second Contrast: The "Unrighteous Mammon" and "That Which Is True"

We have studied the first of the three contrasts or antitheses that our Lord is giving us: "the little, the much." The little are the material things of life, the much are the spiritual things.

The second antithesis or contrast is given in verse 11. Jesus says, "If you are or did not become faithful in the unrighteous or the unjust mammon, you will not be faithful in that which is true." This is the contrast between the unrighteous mammon and that which is true. Our Lord has told us that there are relative values that we must place on material things and on spiritual things. He has called material things of little value, and He has called spiritual things of much value and now, they are the real thing He says.

Interestingly enough, we find this word mammon used only in one other instance in the New Testament, in Matthew 6:24. It is part of the Sermon on the Mount. "No one can have, or can serve two masters," our Lord says. Observe that He gives personality to that which we call mammon: personalities, masters, those things that can govern your life. For, He says, you will hate the one and the other you will love. Actually the translation here should be "You would be attached to the one and you will reject the other."

A Misunderstanding of Our Lord's Use of the Word "Hate"

The use of the words hate and reject should not be taken at their face value here, but only as indicating a contrast. It doesn't mean that you should hate all material things—such as food and water. It doesn't mean that you should hate your paycheck every time you receive it, but give it its proper value. The word "hate," as used by our Master, has been greatly misunderstood, especially in Luke 14:26: "If one comes unto me and does not *hate* his father, and mother, and wife, and children, and brethren, and sisters, yea, and his own life also, he cannot be my disciple." This is the exact word found in Matthew 6 dealing with the two masters, telling us we should hate the one and love the other, be attached to one and reject the other. Now, does this word hate, in connection with following Jesus Christ, mean I as a believer must hate my mother in the sense that we understand the word? Must I hate my brother, my wife or my husband, my children, and my own life? Is this what is meant by being a Christian? This gives rise to a misunderstanding in the minds of many unbelievers who say, "I don't want a Christianity that teaches hate. Jesus teaches that I should hate my family, and everything material." Mind you, this is one of the most difficult verses of the New Testament. How are we to understand it?

How to Be a Balanced Christian

For the solution of this problem there are two things I want to point out to you. First, look at verse 33. In between verses

168

26 and 33 there are two parables, the Parable of the Building of the Tower and the Parable of the Warring King. All these words given by our Lord are illustrations. "Now," He says, "don't start building a tower unless you know that you can finish it. Never leave anything half done. Don't go out to fight against the king who comes against you with 20,000 men if you only have 10,000. Be sure you have everything that is necessary to win before you fight against him. Complete the job, if you would be My disciple."

Now observe verse 33: "Thus, therefore, every one of you who does not forsake [apotassetai, the same basic word tassoo from which hupotassoo, 'to subject,' is derived] that does not put away from him his own belongings, that which belongs to him . . . ." What does He mean by "put away from him"? Well, it is absolutely necessary for us to see, if we are going to live our lives in a manner that we shall be thankful for in eternity, that we must strike a proper balance between the value of material things, including relatives and friends, and the Lord Jesus Christ and eternal realities. How to be a balanced Christian is the subject that concerns us.

We are thankful that our Father in heaven realizes we are made of flesh, passions, appetites, propensities that are physical, but at the same time that we possess a soul, a spirit, a mind that must direct these to be used for that which is real, for that which is of greater value. In the New Testament our Lord was always contrasting values, and we derive joy, peace, and blessedness as a result of the true evaluation of things and persons. It is absolutely impossible for us to be really joyful, really blessed, without true values.

Now, in connection with Luke 14:26, where our Lord tells us that we should hate our father and our mother and our children and so on, He does not really mean that we should hate our relatives and all material things, and He classifies these together, because down in verse 33 of that chapter we find our Lord saying, "Thus every one of you, unless he forsakes all that belongs to him . . . ."

Placing Things in Their Proper Category

The word forsake there is actually "put away from him and place them in their proper category." Things, whatever belongs to you, have their place. They may not be great, but they are not nothing. You need food to eat, you need work, you need human companionship.

Now, if you go back to verse 26 you will see that He not only speaks about hating your relatives but also about hating your own life. Here is where a great misunderstanding can occur, "hating your own life," because the Greek word for life there is not life at all, it is *psychee,* meaning "soul." And the word soul refers to the lower instincts of man. It refers to that which makes you cognizant of your environment, while the spirit, *pneuma,* connects you to that which is higher. So when the Lord says you should hate your own soul, He means that which drags you down to the place where you place so much importance on material things, you become like an animal. And He says you must hate all that, you must hate your lower instincts.

A Further Insight Into Our Lord's Use of the Word "Hate"

Actually the word hate must be interpreted in view of what our Lord tells us in another passage of Scripture, and that is Matthew 10:37. This is the parallel in Scripture that we find in Matthew: "He that loveth [keeps on loving, in the Greek] father or mother more than me is not worthy of me: and he that loveth son or daughter more than me is not worthy of

170

me." The word for love here is *phileoo* or *philoon*. It means "He who holds the same interests as his father or mother, above me, is not worthy of me." He who places the interests of his father or mother above those of the Lord is not worthy of Him.

Now, you see here a contrast, a comparison. He doesn't say to forget, forsake, or disregard your father and mother. Of course not. Didn't the Lord say, "Honour thy father and thy mother" (Mark 19:19)? And Ephesians 6:2 repeats this and calls it "the first commandment with promise." Didn't our Lord on the cross look at His mother and say to His disciple John, "Behold thy mother!" (John 19:27). He never taught hatred in the sense we understand it, against parents, children, human relatives, all the belongings of life, or our body, our soul which means our lower instinct. His meaning was, "Give them their proper place. Evaluate them for what they are worth. If you don't, they will deceive you."

Now observe that He calls all this "the unrighteous or the unjust mammon." If you give it more than it deserves, it will deceive you. And one of the greatest dangers that we face in our Christian lives is for persons or things to assume far greater value than they have. Even father or mother or children or husband or wife, or material things, can never do for you what God, what Jesus Christ, can do for you. You see, they belong to different categories. Recognize the categories to which they belong, and give them their proper due.

In the next chapter, I would like to explain how this unrighteous mammon tries to deceive us by making the material, including human relationships, the most important to us, that to which we give our greatest attention and concern. Who of us can say that we really place the spiritual, that which is true, above everything else in life? All else perishes except God himself.

171

THINK IT OVER

1. Explain what our Lord meant when He said that to follow Him we must "hate" our relatives and our own life. (Matthew 10:37 will help to clear up what He means by this.)

2. How can we achieve a proper balance between earthly "loves" and our "love of God"?

3. What did our Lord mean by "the unrighteous mammon"?

4. What did He mean by the contrasting words, "that which is true"?

25

How Mammon
Distorts Our Values

Let us look a little closer at this fellow called the unjust mammon. Who is he? Well, some people say he was a god, or the imitation of a god, in ancient times who represented material things. And our Lord is warning us here to watch out lest the material things of life, that which we can see, may appear to us as a personality, a person.

The Danger of Making an "It" Into a Person

This is one of the most dangerous distortions that can take place in our lives. We mistake the outward aspect of something for an inner reality that does not exist. You don't believe this is serious? What is breaking up marriages today? Exactly that. A man looks at a woman and says, "How beautiful she is!" And he divorces his wife and marries the other woman, not for what she is, but for her beauty—a quality, a thing. Or you look at a man and say, "Boy, he is the head of his corporation, he's got dough." And you marry a person for the material things he possesses, for that which you can see. When you have a wedding, a marriage, a union between a person and a thing, it can't stand. Eventually the thing will disappear, and once the thing depreciates in value, that person is gone. You see how dangerous it is when you have an "it" becoming a "he" or a "she."

And it is even worse when something that is material, something that is ephemeral, something that is passing becomes your god. You fall down and worship something which, not being a real person, can do nothing for you. This is why, when you have trouble, and you are married to a person who has turned from a "he" to an "it," there is no response to your sorrow, no response to your joy. There is no real fellowship between you two, and therefore a break comes.

It is that much worse if an "it" becomes your god. This is exactly what concerned our Lord in the 6th chapter of the Gospel of Matthew in the Sermon on the Mount. In verse 19 He says, "Lay not up treasures for youselves upon earth," as if that was everything in life. Why? Because they may be eaten up by moths or rust, or somebody may come and steal them. In other words, they're not permanent.

The Fallacy of Trying to Serve God and Mammon at the Same Time

Then in Matthew 6: 24 we come to one of the few places that we find again this fellow, mammon. Our Lord says, "No man can serve or be a slave to two masters." What does He mean? You cannot be a slave to material things and at the same time serve the true God. Now, He doesn't mean that you don't need that which is material. But the material never should become your god, your master. You should be its master. If you try to make both the material things of life and God your master, you know who is going to win, don't you? Every time, the material things which you can see and feel, in spite of the fact that they are temporal, will gain priority because that which you cannot see seems unreal. Our Lord says, "For the one you will hate and the other you will love."

The Antidote to the Allurements of the Unrighteous Mammon

Now note verse 31. When you refuse to allow the mammon of unrighteousness to become your god then you will not be anxious saying, "What are we going to eat, or what are we going to drink, or how are we going to be dressed?" So often the inner qualities of life are eaten up by the concerns of the outside man. "After all these things do the heathen, the unbelievers, seek," warns Jesus. And then in verse 33 He gives the proper attitude for the believer: "Seek ye first the kingdom of God and his righteousness." And give as little value as is proper, as it deserves, to the material things of life. Never give it first place. Give it its proper value, and you will never regret it. Then "things" won't control you, won't direct your life, but you will direct them. Don't make the mammon of unrighteousness your God is what our Lord meant.

THINK IT OVER

1. Explain how outward appearances can lead us to make an "it" into a person.
2. What is the fallacy that so-called "Sunday Christians" are committing? (See Matthew 6:24.)
3. Commit Matthew 6:33 to memory as an antidote to worry and a guide to true values.

26

The True Riches

If you go back for a moment to Luke 16:8, you will find that our Lord commended the steward, the economist of "unrighteousness" (which we explained stands for money). He managed his employer's money. Why did the Lord commend him? Because he used money in a proper manner. And of course, in this whole parable the implication is that the rich man was unrighteous. What did he do that was wrong? He dismissed his good worker, his steward, on a false accusation that he was wasting his money. In other words, he was unjust because he was more concerned about the preservation of his money than he was about the wrong done to an individual person. As an old proverb has it, "When money speaks, the truth is silent." This is injustice, this is unrighteousness.

And our Lord continues to say here that whenever we put money first in our lives, when material things occupy the first place and become our master, then in order to preserve that which we have made our master, we will do all kinds of things that may be unjust toward real people. Which is more important in our lives—money, material things, or people?

The Tragedy When Love of Money Supersedes Love of Family

The Greeks have a special word for family love. It is *storgee*. In fact, the Greeks have four different words for love in their language: *Eros,* which is sensual love; *philia,* which is love that is the result of common interests; *agapee,* the love that sees the need in another person and meets that need; and that is the love of God, of course. And the fourth is *storgee,* which refers to family love. It is translated in II Timothy 3:3 as "natural affection," the kind of love that in the last days people shall lack: "family love," the word is *astorgoi*—"without family love." Now, which is more important —to love money or to love your own family?

I heard of a father who was in the basement of his daughter's house trying to fix something for her, when the blow torch exploded and he was badly burned. As if that was not enough, the daughter is suing her father for damages to get all the money that she can out of him. Well, you see this is a perfect illustration of what happens when you put money, material things, first in your life.

Listen, you can't hug money. Money can't answer to your call and say, "I love you"; money can't respond and say, "I love you, too." This is the whole story. Don't make money, that which is not responsive to your heart, to your life, your primary concern in life. It can meet your need but it cannot comfort you; it is not like the true thing of life, the love of God shed abroad in our hearts toward Himself and others. This is the contrast we have here. A person, money, material things always try to appear as if they can meet the whole need of a human being, as if they were God.

178

The Parable of the Rich Farmer

And what more perfect illustration do we have of this than in the 12th chapter of Luke, where the Lord gave us the Parable of the Rich Farmer. What was wrong with this man? He was very successful. God isn't against success, as long as you use its products rightfully. But be careful lest your success becomes your failure. Observe what this farmer said in verse 19: "Soul, thou hast much goods laid up for many years; take thine ease, eat, drink, and be merry." There is one thing that he failed to recognize, that money, the abundance of material things, does not make a person that which he innately was meant by God to be. It does not necessarily indicate God's blessing upon his life. He who can differentiate between that which is not true, that which passes away, that which cannot meet the need of the soul of man and that which can really meet his soul's need, is a wise person.

THINK IT OVER

1. Have you ever been in a situation where you had to make a decision between your concern for money versus your concern for seeing that justice was done to another individual?
2. Who, in the Parable in Luke 16:1-9, made the wrong decision? What was it, and why?
3. Do you know of situations where love of money has broken up "family love"?
4. Name 3 valuable things that money cannot buy.

27

The Third Contrast: What Is "Truly Ours" and What Is "Really Not Ours"

The first contrast our Lord gave us was between that which is least and that which is much (Luke 16:10). The second contrast was between the unrighteous mammon and that which is true (v. 11). The third and last contrast occurs in verse 12. I'm translating from my Greek New Testament: "And if you did not become faithful to that which is another's, somebody else's, who will give you that which is yours?"

The Deception of Thinking We Own "Things"

Interesting, isn't it? The Lord says there are things that are not yours, although you possess them, and there are things that are or can be truly yours. It's a fascinating contrast. What did He mean by it? He's pointing out the deception under which we labor when we think that what we hold in our hands is truly ours. Don't we often say, "Oh, don't touch this; this is *mine*"—whatever the item may be? True, it may be ours now, but it may not be after awhile, especially when there are so many people in our world who say, "What is yours is mine, if I can get it."

What Is Truly Ours?

What is truly ours? Well, to make it very simple, may I say that is truly ours which death cannot take away, which others cannot steal, which moth and rust cannot corrupt. What should we consider important in life? That which no one can take from us. It is a distinction between those things that are ours that we can lose, and that which is ours that we cannot lose.

I remember the story of a poor man who had his meager lunch stolen by one of his fellow workers. Hungry after the lunch hour, he sang and praised the Lord, and they made fun of him. They said, "My goodness, your very lunch has been stolen away from you and you're praising God. What for? You're nuts!" "Oh, no," he said, "I'm not nuts. They may have stolen my lunch, but they couldn't steal my appetite from me." Have we ever though of that? Which is more important, hunger, that inbuilt valve within us that makes our body able and eager to eat, or just the food that lasts us only a little while? Which is truly ours?

Something No One Can Ever Take from Us

The Apostle Paul, in the 8th chapter of Romans, presents this truth vividly in verses 33 through 39. Whenever you have something stolen from you, whenever you have even the most beloved person taken away from you in this life, when you lose everything that is attached to you and not part of you, read these verses:

"Who shall lay any thing to the charge of God's elect? It is God that justifieth. Who is he that condemneth? It is Christ

182

that died, yea rather, that is risen again, who is even at the right hand of God, who also maketh intercession for us. Who shall separate us from the love of Christ? [And the question is, is the love of Christ more important to us than anything else? That is truly ours, and nobody can take it from us; it is part of us.] shall tribulation, or distress, or persecution, or famine, or nakedness, or peril, or sword?"

The things that are attached to us can be taken away from us, but the love of Christ within us, no one can take. "As it is written, For thy sake we are killed all the day long; we are accounted as sheep for the slaughter. Nay, in all these things we are more than conquerors through him that loved us. For I am persuaded, that neither death, nor life, nor angels, nor principalities, nor powers, nor things present, nor things to come, nor height, nor depth, nor any other creature, shall be able to separate us from the love of God, which is in Christ Jesus, our Lord." Almost everything else, except what God does as His perfect work through the Holy Spirit in our heart, is deficient, is transitory, is temporary. The love of God can be ours for eternity.

And you remember the whole basic lesson here is that we are to use that which is least, use that which is really not ours and we are only stewards thereof, so that we may have a welcoming committee in heaven. You cannot serve two masters, for while your attachment to one increases, your attachment to the other decreases. Choose God, or the things of this world will become a consuming fire within you.

Making It Practical

Read Habakkuk 3:17, 18, and try paraphrasing it as a Christian friend of mine did recently:

1. Although I shall not enjoy good health . . .

183

2. Although all my dearest loved ones shall be taken from me—by death or by circumstances . . .
3. Although my bank accounts, or Social Security, or pension shall fail . . .
4. Although I shall suffer the excruciating pain of a terminal illness . . .
5. Although I shall have to go to a hospital or nursing home to end my days—and leave my own dear home and familiar surroundings . . .

"Yet I will rejoice in the Lord, I will joy in the God of my salvation."

And she appended these verses:

"The Lord gave, and the Lord hath taken away; blessed be the name of the Lord" (Job 1:21b).

"Though he slay me, yet will I trust in him" (Job 13:15).

"For he hath said, I will never leave thee, nor forsake thee" (Heb. 13:5b).

"That's the bottom line," she commented. "God help me to live up to it!"

THINK IT OVER

1. Are your material possessions truly yours: your home, your bank account, or even your family?
2. Explain briefly what our Lord meant by the things that are truly ours.
3. On which are you placing the highest value? Can you affirm the words of Habakkuk 3:17, 18 as they might apply to your own circumstances in life?

184

28

Have Only One Master

This parable about how to manage money given by our Lord in Luke 16:1-9 applies to Christians only. They live on earth in view of heaven. The unbeliever considers everything as having its beginning and ending on earth. For the believer in Jesus Christ, however, how he manages his money, and generally his life, affects the measure of his enjoyment of his after-life. How a believer spends his money is important not only in obtaining benefits in this life but also in eternity.

The most important use of the Christian's money after his basic needs are cared for is to lead souls to Jesus Christ who, upon his departure from this life, will constitute his welcoming comittee in heaven.

Don't Overvalue Little Things

There is the danger that if we are not careful as Christians, we will allow the development of a philosophy of life which may deceive us by attributing more value to the little things of life than they are worth. All material things are of small value compared to our spiritual riches in and through Christ. In His Sermon on the Mount, the Lord very clearly stated what is the fate of earthly treasures: "Lay not up for yourselves treasures upon earth, where moth and rust doth corrupt, and where thieves break through and steal" (Matt. 6:19). There are no "if's and but's" about it. Treasures lose their value. If you use them, however, to accumulate treasures in heaven, then their full value becomes permanent and eternal and multiplies. Our Lord further said, "Where your treasure is, there will your heart be also" (Matt. 6:21). If your heart is in heaven, then you will see to it that your money gets you a welcoming committee in heaven through using it to preach the Gospel and to win souls which actually will be your treasure in heaven.

Therefore, don't allow the little, material things of life to accomplish little only. Let your money proclaim to individuals that their debts, or sins, can be forgiven even as the steward did.

The contrast our Lord wants to draw with this pronouncement about "having two masters" in Matthew 6:24 and Luke 16:13 is between the temporary and the eternal accomplishments of money or material things. Money has no intrinsic value. It is only good as to the extent it can serve your life. What good is gold to the hungry man when there is no food to buy? None of us would want to be a King Midas and have *everything* we touch turn to gold. Its true value must be gauged by what necessities it can buy to sustain life. Money can buy necessities for life on earth, but life on earth is temporary. One day, sooner or later, death will come, and anything money can do in order that it may provide satisfaction in eternity is to be considered as of greater value.

Many thrilling stories have been told about the Klondike gold rush, but one is most impressive and instructive.

A prospecting party, penetrating far into the Klondike,

came upon a miner's hut. Upon entering, they found the frozen bodies of two men and a large quantity of gold. On a table there was a letter which told of the successful search for the precious ore. In their eagerness to mine the gold as quickly as possible and before anybody else came and discovered it, the miners had neglected to make provision for the coming of winter. Each day the two men gleefully uncovered gold in abundance. One morning they awoke to find that a blizzard had come. For days the tempest raged. Escape was beyond hope and soon their little store of food and fuel was gone. After writing their letter, they lay down to die in the midst of abounding gold!

The miner's folly was not in finding and gathering the gold, but in neglecting to provide for the coming winter.

How like those who make no provision for the coming winter of death. That's the subject of the parable our Lord gave: "Get ready for your metastasis while you have time. Win souls for heaven while still on earth and acting as a steward of Christ's forgiveness."

THINK IT OVER

1. How can we increase the value of our money?
2. What contrast was our Lord making in Matthew 6:24 and Luke 16:13?
3. Does money have intrinsic value in itself? Give an illustration to substantiate your answer.
4. What is its true value?

29

Preparation for Our Home in Heaven

Money can buy a luxurious home here on earth, but how long shall one be able to live in that luxurious home? It is only temporary. Now, I don't believe that the Lord wants us to live in physical misery on earth and expose ourselves to disease and unnecessary suffering of our own making. But while we build our earthly house of clay, let us remember that our choice of the disposition of our earthly material goods becomes the construction blocks of our home in heaven. Will it be a hut or a mansion? Christian, stop to compare how much of your money is spent on earthly, and many times, unnecessary luxuries and how much on winning friends who would welcome you into heaven. The mansion here is for now, but the mansion in heaven is for our eternal existence.

Matthew gives the important pronouncement of our Lord about having two masters in a very fitting context. It would really make more consecutive reading if Matthew 6:24 were to follow verses 19 to 21:

"Lay not up for yourselves treasures upon earth, where moth and rust doth corrupt, and where thieves break through and steal:

"But lay up for yourselves treasures in heaven, where neither moth nor rust doth corrupt, and where thieves do not break through nor steal:

"For where your treasure is, there will your heart be also."

Two principles are clearly enunciated here:

1. Money can be of only temporary value if it is used to procure things for this world.

2. If your money is used to buy things only for this earth, your heart will be enslaved by the earth. What your money will buy for heaven will be of no consequence to you.

To the above, immediately add the words of Christ in verse 24:

"No man can serve two masters: for either he will hate the one, and love the other; or else he will hold to the one, and despise the other. Ye cannot serve God and mammon."

We come to the obvious conclusion that if material things become your mammon, your god with a small g, then you are no more the master of your money, but its slave. You may find by and by that you haven't sent enough building materials to heaven beforehand and have only a basement instead of a mansion. How you manage your money is your choice, but the consequences of that choice are predetermined. You cannot spend the money which could and should be winning souls to Christ on unnecessary, earthly luxuries and expect a large welcoming committee and reward in heaven.

Surely Luke could not have put this pronouncement of our Lord at a more appropriate place than at the end of this parable concerning one's money and position in life.

Cautiously View Material Things

We should view material things with great caution as they tend to become our god, our mammon, in life. They assume greater importance than they deserve while spiritual riches tend to be pushed to the background. The reversal of importance is done very subtly.

God will test you in how you use material things. How you manage your money tells whether you can be entrusted with the management of important and valuable spiritual truths.

THINK IT OVER

1. Give two principles found in Matthew 6:19-21.
2. Is it really possible for money and material things to enslave us? How?
3. Are we free to choose the consequences of our choice?

30

We Cannot Have Two
Heads on One Body

Before William Carey, the great pioneer missionary to India, left England to serve God in that far-off land, he was a shoemaker. His soul was so filled with the love of God that he went about preaching the Gospel from village to village.

One day a friend came to him and said, "Mr. Carey, I want to speak to you very seriously."

"Well," said Mr. Carey, "what is it?"

The friend replied, "By your traveling about preaching as you do, you are neglecting your business. If you only gave more attention to your business, you would soon move ahead and prosper, but as it is you are simply neglecting your business."

"Neglecting my business?" said Carey. "My business is to extend the Kingdom of God. I only cobble shoes to pay expenses."

We said in the previous chapter that it would help us to understand Christ's pronouncement about having two masters if we placed Matthew 6:24 immediately after verses 19 to 21. And yet there is a reason why Matthew has verses 22 and 23 in between, for they speak of the eye and how it can be deceived by that which glitters and shines.

"The light of the body is the eye: if therefore thine eye be single, thy whole body shall be full of light.

"But if thine eye be evil, thy whole body shall be full of darkness. If therefore the light that is in thee be darkness, how great is that darkness!"

The Lord wanted to stress that the condition of our eyesight affects the value we attribute to material things.

The eye of a carnal Christian finds greater satisfaction in the physical aspects of life than in the spiritual. Does a luxurious way of life or the testimony of a soul saved from sin and moral degradation bring greater joy to your heart? Do you find more pleasure in satisfying your whims and wants which are not really needed for your physical sustenance or in meeting the need of God's work?

Keeping the Balance

Keeping the balance between the physical and the material is our duty. Our Lord ate and drank what was necessary to maintain His physical life. In fact, He was even called "a gluttonous man, and a winebibber" (Matt. 11:19; Luke 7:34). Nevertheless, our Lord really practiced what He preached when He said to the tempting devil in Luke 4:4: "Man shall not live by bread (i.e., physical bread) alone, but by every word of God."

In reality, we are only stewards on this earth. That, however, which we appropriate and receive by faith from Jesus Christ is permanently ours. It cannot be detached from us.

Regarding these attitudes which we must develop toward material things, the Lord gives an axiom, an indisputable, absolute statement in Luke 16:13. The same statement He gave also in Matthew 6:24. Here it is:

"No servant can serve two masters: for either he will hate the one, and love the other; or else he will hold to the one, and despise the other. Ye cannot serve God and mammon."

We Can Have Only One Voice of Authority

Now that verse is pretty authoritarian, isn't it? But Christ ought to know, for He made us. He put one head on each body. You cannot have two presidents with equal power and authority directing one and the same corporation. He made us monocephalous, not dicephalous beings.

Pity the employee who has to take directions from two bosses who are equal in authority but differ in their principles. The most important thing for any corporation to prosper and be successful is to make clear to its employees the chain of command. Otherwise, there is absolute chaos as each one "does his own thing" without the cooperation necessary for a smooth-running organization.

The Christian can only have one boss. That's a sound and practical axiom. Christ has spoken of mammon, the god of money in the two passages, Matthew 6:24 and Luke 16:9, 11, and 13. Both passages deal with the comparative values of material and spiritual things. The reason for this is because it is so easy for us to wittingly or unwittingly allow these material things of so little importance to become our god and the ruler of our lives. Be sure that Christ will not be satisfied with second place in your heart and life. He who offers God a second place offers Him no place at all.

If you allow this, then the necessary consequence is that God will be displaced by mammon. A body has to have a head, be it good or bad, but it cannot have one which is good and one which is bad. There is only one throne in your heart. It cannot be occupied by two kings of equal authority and importance. If you try to accommodate two kings on one and the same throne, you will be utterly confused. Civil war will ensue. You won't know whom to please. Pause to think. Your confusion in life may be totally due to this abnormality in your life. You are one body with two heads.

At one time my wife and I saw a little two-headed turtle on display. It was fascinating to watch as each little head tried to pull its cumbersome shell in the opposite direction. Believe me, it didn't get very far. Strain and pull, strain and pull, and yet, there it sat worn out by its efforts against itself. Whoever said two heads are better than one hadn't seen that poor, little schizophrenic turtle.

THINK IT OVER

1. Why did Matthew speak of the eye when he was giving Christ's pronouncement that a man cannot have two masters?
2. Is it possible to always obey two voices of equal authority?
3. Could this be one reason God entrusted authority in one person in a marriage relationship?
4. What happens when both parents claim equal authority and yet disagree on how to raise a child?
5. Name a very possible cause of confusion and frustration in one's life.
6. Are two heads always better than one?

31

Everybody Has a Master

The only difference between Matthew 6:24 and Luke 16:13 is that in Matthew 6:24, it does not say, "No *servant* can serve two masters," but "No *man* can serve two masters." We don't have to be in a position of servitude to have a master. Every human being, no matter what his economic or sociological position, has to have someone who is over him to be his master. We never can be the complete master of ourselves although we may try. Someone or something is in control. We cannot be master of our own selves and at the same time have God as our master. We, being the church, are the body, the bride; and Christ is the head, the groom, the boss. The real danger is that the god of this material world, the unjust mammon, may become our god, our master. Then God cannot be master of our lives anymore.

The Lord does not enforce Himself as anybody's master. As the bride of Christ, we install Him as such the same as the bride of today willingly and cheerfully places herself under the protective and loving headship of her husband. The day

197

will come when He will subjugate everybody and everything (I Cor. 15:24-26). But for now, He is a reigning King by invitation and voluntary obedience only.

Examine yourself seriously. Who is master of your life—the unrighteous mammon, or God, the giver and sustainer of your life, the giver of all good and perfect gifts?

Whether one is a servant or not makes no difference. Rich or poor, an employer or an employee, all are under authority. There is nobody in this world who is not. For the servant it is more obvious that he is under authority, but for the master of the servant, it is not. However, the wealthy person is always in danger of concluding that he is self-sufficient and self-dependent.

You Choose to Serve

In Luke 16:13, the word translated "servant" is *oiketees* in Greek. This Greek word occurs four times in the New Testament, namely, Acts 10:7; Romans 14:1; I Peter 2:18 and here in Luke 16:13. This is the basic word from which *oikonomos,* "steward" (Luke 16:1, 3, 8) comes. It is derived from *oikos,* "house," and the verb *nemoo,* "to administer, to manage." *Oiketees* is "one dwelling or belonging to a house." It also came to mean a domestic servant. He is not a slave, however, such as *doulos,* as opposed to a free man, *elephtheros* (I Cor. 12:13; Rev. 13:16; 19:18).

Oiketees, "a house servant," does not bring out and emphasize the servile relation so strongly as *doulos,* "bond servant," does. The house servant is one of the household, of the family, not one necessarily born in the house, (*oikogenees*). He works in the house, but he is a free man. It is his freedom in service that is characteristic of the word. Sometimes there can be a serving wife or child. *Oiketees,* therefore, means "a free servant." He is a servant who chooses to serve and he

198

continues to serve at will. He does not have to accept a master imposed upon him. He chooses his master and the household he will serve.

Jesus Christ Will Not Force Us to Serve Him

Jesus Christ is not speaking about the homage or acknowledgement of God which man will be forced to avow one day. Isaiah 45:23 tells us "I have sworn by myself, the word is gone out of my mouth in righteousness, and shall not return, That unto me every knee shall bow, every tongue shall confess." Yes, the Lord will one day be master of all whether we want it or not. But in Matthew 6:24, Christ is speaking about voluntary service.

As someone said: "Giving grudgingly or of necessity reminds me of a farmer's cow."

"How much milk does that cow give?" a friend asked the farmer.

"Well," replied the farmer, "if you mean by voluntary contribution, she doesn't give any. But if you can get her cornered so she can't kick to hurt anybody, an able-bodied man can take away about eleven quarts of milk a day from her."

See how beautifully our freedom to choose our master in this life is expressed. We are not born slaves to God. We were born free to choose when God originally made us. We may choose to disobey our Maker's explicit command. Ever since that original disobedience, men have been born sinners (Romans 5:12). But God sheds His light upon every man coming into the world (John 1:9). The choice to accept or reject that light is every man's. But we cannot simultaneously choose to be the servant of God and the world, the servant of light and darkness. You travel either to the West or to the East. You cannot simultaneously move in both directions.

199

Either you are saved or you are a sinner. As a saved servant, you have God on the throne and you worship Him. As a sinner servant, you worship the god of this material world, mammon.

THINK IT OVER

1. What is the difference between Matthew 6:24 and Luke 16:13?
2. To what type of a servant does Luke 16:13 refer?
3. What kind of service is Christ speaking about in these verses?
4. Is it possible for a man to be both a servant of God and a slave of the world?

32

Every Person Needs a Master

Man may occupy the lowest place or the most exalted in life. It makes no difference. He is so constituted that he must belong to someone. A husband belongs to his wife. A wife belongs to her husband. Children belong to their parents. The sense of belonging is essential to human happiness. Man needs someone to be attached to, someone to look up to other than himself. He needs a controlling force in his life. That is the basic declaration implied in the words of Jesus of whom it is said, "All things were made by him; and without him was not anything made that was made" (John 1:3). The Greek text does not say "all things," but *panta,* "all," both people and things, everything as an individual and the entire universe in its cohesiveness and totality.

"No one can have two masters" is what Matthew 6:24 declares. The Greek word is *oudeis,* made up of the conjunction *oude,* "not even," and *eis,* "one." In other words, not one single person can have two masters. That is the negative way of saying we need a master, but two we cannot have. Christ did not imply that we need no master, but that we need only one, otherwise we would be what James calls a two-souled man (James 1:8 and 4:8). The word here is *dipsychos,* "double souled," translated "double minded." The division of our soul and mind between two opposing forces is impossible. We cannot have one pulling us by the hands and another by the feet in two opposing directions and still survive. It is either God or mammon, God or the world.

We Cannot Have Two First's

The words of Christ can be very easily misunderstood. Does He really expect us to hate the world in which we live? Does He expect us to hate our relatives as He said in Luke 14:26 and Matthew 10:37? Listen to His words in both of these verses:

"If any man (observe how all-inclusive is His statement) come to me, and hate not his father, and mother, and wife, and children, and brethren, and sisters, yea, and his own life (*psychee,* that element of his personality dragging him down to the animal level) also, he cannot be my disciple."

Now listen how Matthew rendered it:

"He that loveth father or mother more than me is not worthy of me: and he that loveth son or daughter more than me is not worthy of me."

The verb hate must be given the meaning of "loving more." Christ was saying in essence, "You cannot love any human relative or any material possession or pleasure more than you love Me. You cannot place Me on the same level as human relationships or material possessions. I am God. I am your Maker, not merely your relation or your possession. I am the only master deserving to be had by you."

Anyone else or anything else demanding to be your master is a usurper, a deceiver. He or it will utterly disappoint you.

That we need a master there is no doubt. But we must watch whom we make our master. If we make the wrong person or thing or pursuit our master, the real need in our

202

lives will never be met. That does not mean that we do not need relatives and possessions and some pleasures found in this world. After all, God is responsible for creating family ties and possessions to be had by us. But we cannot allow anyone or anything to take the place which belongs exclusively to God. We need God first plus our relatives and possessions. He is the "one" before what otherwise would be nothing, a "zero." If life has been empty, it may be because we have eliminated the Number One which makes the otherwise zeroes of value and therefore we have but emptiness. There is a difference between $1,000,000 and $0,000,001. Our true wealth or utter poverty depends on how far in front we put God or how far behind. We are either millionaires or possess but a fraction of it.

Christians sometimes misunderstand the concept of disciple-ship. They interpret it as a process of giving up selective things. One day we give up this and another day something else and use the money for God. But what we need to give up is not things, but self. Only then things cannot become our mammon. We must ever be on guard, for it is possible to give up things and, by so doing, think we are giving up self which may be far from the truth.

Didn't the Lord state it most clearly in Matthew 6:33, "Seek ye first the kingdom of God, and his righteousness; and all these things shall be added unto you"? And after the Lord spoke about His providential physical care of His creation and the parable of the prosperous successful rich farmer in Luke 12:31, He said, "But rather seek ye the kingdom of God; and all these things shall be added unto you." Interestingly enough, the verb translated "seek ye", *zeeteite,* in Greek is in the second person plural present imperative which implies continuous seeking, not a once-and-for-all affair.

Christ Claims Preeminent Position in Our Lives

The danger of putting relatives and possessions first is ever present in our Christian lives. The Lord is not addressing

203

unbelievers on any of these occasions. In the Sermon on the Mount, He was giving His disciples the laws of discipleship (see Matthew 5:1). On the occasion of Luke 12:31, He was speaking to His disciples (see Luke 12:1). And on the occasion of Luke 16:13, our Lord was speaking to His disciples (see Luke 16:1). He knew full well that those who were not His disciples had a master and that was mammon. He was the master of the rich man, the employer in the parable of Luke 16:1-9 who dismissed his business manager on mere hearsay. Money was the rich man's master, his god. Otherwise, he would not have acted so unjustly against a faithful, hard-working steward whom the Lord so explicitly commended in Luke 16:8.

But the Lord said that you, as His disciples, can only have one master, Jesus Christ Himself, God. No pronouncements of our Lord other than the ones we referred to in Luke 14:26 and Matthew 10:37 are as explicit about His uniqueness as God in the sense that He is the only deserving master. Either you put Christ first or you will never experience His true value in your life. No "if's or but's" about it. If you are living in spiritual poverty, it is due to the fact that you may have put someone else or something else first in your life, no matter who or what. Listen to Christ speak: "If anyone comes to *me*"—He does not say "to the Father"—"He cannot be my disciple," not "Father's disciple." "And whosoever doth not bear his cross, and come after *me*, cannot be *my* disciple," not God's disciple, but "*my* disciple." Can there be any doubt that He was consciously declaring who He was, namely God in the flesh?

THINK IT OVER

1. Does God really expect us to hate our families?

2. What does this verse mean?
3. Is giving up things a sufficient sacrifice for our Savior?
4. What does He really want us to give Him?

33

The Day of Judgment of the Christian's Works

There is a fundamental difference between Christianity and other religions.

Christianity is a living Christ who demands to be absolute master of our lives. He did not remain in the grave, but He arose from the dead. He lives and follows all our labor for Him. He records all our works in the books of life referred to in Revelation 20:12. There is the book of life in which are written the names of the redeemed (Phil. 4:3; Rev. 3:5; 5:1-9; 13:8; 17:8; 21:27), and in Revelation 20:21 we have both the book of life and the books. While the Book of Life is where the names of the redeemed are written, the books of life are those books by which the dead are going to be judged for their faithfulness and fruitfulness. "And the dead were judged out of those things which were written in the books, according to their works."

Do you realize that as every accountant keeps books in which are recorded all the transactions of business, so is the living Lord keeping books? All the entries are true. There can be no falsification of the facts. Aren't you glad that everything you do for the Lord, no matter how insignificant, is recorded by Him? Also everything you fail to do which you could have done and which could have resulted in welcoming friends in heaven will be recorded.

This picture of the master and the steward or business manager in the parable of the unjust businessman is most suggestive. It brings eternity down to the most practical level so we cannot miss the implications.

You and I are stewards. We manage money entrusted to us by our Master. Of course, we cannot equate God with this rich man of our parable except in some specific aspects. As the rich man fired his business manager without forewarning, so the Lord sets the time of our metastasis, our removal from this earth. His decision for our metastasis is deliberately arrived at, not on the basis of false accusation, but on His absolute knowledge of our future inclinations toward Him. As the decision of the rich man to fire his steward was sudden and irreversible, so is God's decision for our metastasis in most instances.

When the rich man learned of the accusation against his steward that he had wasted his belongings, he asked for an accounting, and so will our Lord.

An Accounting Expected

The word used for this accounting in Greek is intriguing. Look at Luke 16:2. "And he (the rich boss) called him, and said unto him (the economist), How is it that I hear this of thee? Give an account of thy stewardship." That word translated "account" in Greek is *logon* (*logos* in the nominative). In modern Greek the meaning of the word has carried through. We call an accountant *logisteen*. It is the same basic word used by John to designate our Lord's preincarnate and eternal state as purely spiritual essence. He was and shall ever be the *Logos,* "the word," which actually means intelligence from which comes "logic". It also means "the expression" of that intelligence in words that can be comprehended by finite humans such as we are. That's what "the Word who became flesh" did for us. He made the infinite and eternal God, who in His essential essence is Spirit and thus incomprehensible to us, comprehensible to us in human words. *Logos* therefore is an explanation.

Now, what we find revealed to us is that on the resurrection of the believers at the *parousia,* at the coming or appearance of our Lord who has been our Master, there will be the opening of the accounting books, the journal of our lives, so to speak, and all the daily entries examined. Then for all that we as believers said and did, there will be demanded an explanation, a *logos.*

The Beema Judgment of Christ

This heavenly Internal Revenue Audit is what is called in the New Testament "The Beema Judgment." It is referred to in Romans 14:10.

"For we shall all stand before the judgment seat of Christ." That expression "judgment seat" is the translation of a single word in Greek, *beema,* which essentially means an elevated seat for a judge or king (Matt. 27:19; John 19:13; Acts 12:21; 25:6, 17). Hence it means a judgment seat; a tribunal. It is the tribunal where an audit of the words and deeds of the Christian is going to be held. Also what was left undone and neglected by each believer is going to be revealed. We are going to find out how well we managed our money and our entire life on earth. This life of ours and this money that is entrusted to us is being managed by us at freedom, but there is going to be an audit by the Living Judge who has recorded everything in the accounting books.

This is only natural. Can you imagine an accountant here on earth not being subject to audit? He could put down anything he chooses. He could cheat. It is the prospect of being checked that keeps him in line. Similarly, it is the prospect of the *beema* judgment of Christ that causes us to a great extent to be diligent about our stewardship, our management, and thus we should be on our guard to be responsible managers of God's trust to us.

If you read further down in what follows Romans 14:10, you will find some startling revelations:

The first is the declaration that the judge is alive. Romans 14:11 says: "For it is written, (Is. 45:23) As I live, saith the Lord, every knee shall bow to me, and every tongue shall confess to God." Does this have to do with unbelievers? Does this refer to the ultimate reconciliation of all men and things to God? Will the Lord force people to do what they never wanted to do on earth? Impossible. Of course, there is going to be a subjugation of those who rejected God in their lives, however not unto salvation but unto judgment and inactivity as far as the further perpetuation of the evil in which they engaged while on earth. This is more clearly referred to by Paul in I Corinthians 15:24-26: "Then cometh the end (the goal of Christ's resurrection. No dead person can do anything), when he shall have delivered up the kingdom to God, even the Father; when he shall have put down all rule and all authority and power. For he must reign, till he hath put all enemies under his feet. The last enemy that shall be destroyed is death." Now, how could a dead Christ do that? Impossible. He is alive! There is no living Mohammed, no living Buddha, no living Confucius. But Jesus is going to preside over the audit of our life management and money because He lives.

When Paul writes in Romans 14:10 "for we shall all stand

before the judgment seat of Christ," he refers to himself and all believers. The theme of Romans 14 is how the stronger Christian brother treats the weaker one who has minor differences with him. Read Romans 14:1-8. Much of the judgment of the *beema* will be concerning our inter-Christian relationships.

Here it is in Romans 14:11: "As I live saith the Lord." He will be at your audit and mine. And then read verse 12: "So then every one of us shall give account of himself to God." The word "account" is *logon* in Greek. You and I will be called upon to give a verbal explanation of our money and life management. It is inescapable.

Now the question is, What if the Lord finds out that we have not acted prudently? Will there be rewards only or punishments also?

You put your arms up and say: "Horror! Punishments in heaven? How can it be?" Well, read the second reference where the *beema* judgment occurs in II Corinthians 5:10: "For we must all appear before the judgment seat of Christ; that every one may receive the things done in his body, according to that he hath done, whether it be good or bad." That last phrase is arresting: "whether it be good or bad." If the *beema* judgment is all for rewards and not for punishments, how can it be that the Just Auditor, the God of righteousness, is going to reward us for the bad things we did while in the body, during our earthly lives? The indubitable conclusion must be that as we are going to be rewarded for the good things done in the flesh, we are going to be punished for the bad things. We cannot be rewarded for the bad things. This is axiomatic; it is self-evident.

The story goes that a millionaire stood at heaven's gate. Being conducted to a small cottage located in the midst of other tiny, unpretentious houses, he complained, "Can it be

211

that I, who have lived in a palace on earth midst scenes of luxury and comfort, must now dwell eternally in this small abode?"

Came the reply, "We built this house out of the material you sent to us while you were on earth. We could have built a palace for you here if you had only sent us the material with which to build it! But it's too late now to improve upon it."

THINK IT OVER

1. What is the difference between the book of life and the books spoken of in Revelation 20:12?
2. Explain what the "word who became flesh" actually did for us.
3. What is the judgment seat referred to in Romans 14:10?
4. At the beema judgment seat, will our good deeds be rewarded and our bad deeds overlooked?

34

What Do the Words
"Bad" and "Good" Really Mean?

\

Permit me to digress a little and explain the real meaning of these two words translated "good" or "bad" which is not readily seen in English and which are found in II Corinthians 5:10: "For we must all appear before the judgment seat of Christ; that every one may receive the things done in his body, according to that he hath done, whether it be good or bad."

In Greek the word for "good" is *agathon*. This means good which does not stop with the doer but which finds its influence in the lives of others. It stands in comparison to *kalon* which means good in oneself or itself without necessarily affecting others or the environment around it. You may be good in yourself (*kalos*—nominative) but not *agathos*, good and influencing for good. Consider the hermit or ascetic who withdraws from society to be alone with God and worship Him. His life may be good, *kalos*, but not *agathos*. It is of no benefit to the masses who need spiritual or physical help and direction. It is *kalos* only. To withdraw from a needy, heartbreaking world, turning a deaf ear to their cries for help, is not being *agathos,* and it is not pleasing to our Lord.

We shall be rewarded as Christians for being not merely good in ourselves. The commendation of our Lord upon the faithful steward was not that he was merely good, that he did no harm to anyone, but that he used his position as a steward, even in view of his forthcoming removal from his job, to influence others. He went to some of his master's debtors and he did them a favor by forgiving part of their indebtedness and he helped his master by collecting at least part of what they owed. There is no indication whatsoever that what he collected he kept in whole or in part. He turned it over to his master. Perhaps in what he did we have a subtle suggestion. As managers of God's grace and forgiveness on earth, we cannot make people accept all that God has to offer. Maybe the part payment by the debtor is meant to indicate our part in working out that which God does for us and in us. Of course, this could not refer to the part unto salvation. The debtor was unable to meet the payment in whole. It could be in the fifty percent for the first debtor and the 80 percent for the second debtor collected we see what Paul calls in Philippians 2:12 the working out of one's salvation. "Work out your own salvation with fear and trembling." Salvation offered by the Lord must be accepted by man. It is His salvation full and free. But then there must be works resulting from that salvation. This is the management of the redeemed life. Some contribute fifty percent and others eighty percent. Isn't it true that there are degrees of fidelity to Jesus Christ in life? We cannot serve two masters, but how many of us try to please mammon as much as we can while we are in the service of the Lord Jesus. What an indictment against us! Let us each examine our own conscience.

Multiplied Benefits

The steward engaged in making friends who would welcome him after he found himself in want and loneliness having been finally removed from his position. Are we going to find ourselves in a similar position after our metastasis, our removal from this earth when our stewardship of the Master's trust is all finished? Of course, in so many ways we fail our Lord that we shall need Him when He sits as our judge to be as liberal and merciful with us as possible. This is what James 2:12, 13 tells us He will be for those who were merciful on earth. Our mercifulness here will find mercy there as our Lord assures us in the fifth beatitude: "Blessed are the merciful: for they shall obtain mercy" (Matt. 5:7).

What will count when we appear at the *beema* judgment is how many souls will be in the eternal habitations who were brought there as a result of our earthly stewardship. That will prove to be the best use of our money. How many sinners, debtors of our Lord, received the forgiveness we offered in His Name? They in turn would use their "mammon of unrighteousness," money which they would have otherwise used for unrighteous purposes, to lead others to Christ who also would constitute our welcoming committee in heaven. It's not only our spiritual children who will welcome us in the eternal habitations, but also our grandchildren and great-grandchildren!

Most of us are familiar with the pyramid selling schemes of certain organizations whereby a person receives a certain percentage of the sales of those signed up under him, thereby increasing the base of his income from each new salesman recruited. This is not such a new idea. It seems God thought of it long before man did.

Thus what counts is not being merely good (*kaloi*), but *agathoi,* influentially good. To have money that is made honestly is not as important as using that money for making friends for Christ. That is, and will prove to be, the most prudent use and management of money.

Bad or Influentially Bad

Now the other word in II Corinthians 5:10 translated "bad" is *kakon.* That means bad in itself in contrast to *poneeron,* influentially bad or evil. The name of the devil is *poneeros* (Matt. 5:39). He is not satisfied in being bad in himself but he is malicious, mischievous in a spiritual sense. The word used in II Corinthians 5:10 to indicate what we as Christians are going to be judged and punished for is *kakon,* just "bad". We, as Christians, don't have to be evil, malicious, purposely harming others. Being bitter, vindictive in the deep recesses of our hearts without seeking or having opportunity to express it, is enough. We shall be judged not only for our evil acts but for our dormant, bad thoughts. Not only how we used the money that we had on earth or our opportunities, but how we would have used money if we had it or opportunities if we had them. That is quite sobering. It should revolutionize our lives.

THINK IT OVER

1. What are the two different shades of meaning of the word "good"?
2. What are the two different shades of meaning of the word "bad"?
3. On the day of the judgement of the Christian's works, who will receive the greatest mercy?

35

An Impossible Situation

The Lord said in Luke 16:13 and Matthew 6:24 that it is absolutely impossible for any of us, either a humble house-servant or the richest person on earth, not to have a master governing us other than ourselves.

Each one of us must choose who is going to be first in his life. It is going to be either God through Jesus Christ or all that is actively opposed to Him, who in this parable in Luke 16:1-13 is called "the unjust mammon." That's the god of material things, the god of this world. It can be your relatives, either all of them together or any one of them, or your possessions. If mammon is truly your master, then God does not reign at all. It's either the one or the other. It cannot be both.

And then in the second part of Christ's declaration, He tells us why it cannot be that two opposing kings may be sitting on the same throne, the throne of your heart: "For either he will hate the one, and love the other; or else he will hold to the one, and despise the other."

The word translated "for" in Greek is *gar*, "because." Here is the reason why you cannot serve two masters. They cannot both be loved by you equally and simultaneously. You cannot have two forces within you in opposition to each other and be able to please them both. How can you live in peace and tranquility if you have two women in your life? One has to suffer and the other gain. But nobody loses more than yourself. Dual fidelity to opposing individuals or forces is torture. That's why so many destroy their marriages today thinking they can love two partners. Take it from Christ. It is absolutely impossible. Sooner or later, you will hate the one and love the other. You may go from one to the other, but then unconsciously you try to live with both hatred and love. You want darkness and light in the same place. It cannot be. You must make your choice. Don't be a fool. You harm others and above all, yourself. The consequence of moral compromise is hate and love springing from the same source. Or as James says in 3:11 and 12: "Doth a fountain send forth at the same place sweet water and bitter? . . . No fountain can both yield salt water and fresh."

There is no doubt as to who these two masters are referred to by our Lord. The one is the Lord God, equated as deserving first place in Luke 14:26 and Matthew 10:37. And the other is mammon. This we find at the end of Luke 16:13 and Matthew 6:24.

Actually in order to understand the pronouncement more clearly, we should put it this way:

"No servant or no one can serve two masters."

Why?

Because they are opposing each other:

"Ye cannot serve God and mammon."

And since they oppose each other, one of them will be hated and the other will be loved.

Therefore, don't put yourself in such an embarrassing position of self-destruction.

Whose Bond Slave Are We?

The verb which is used as an infinitive in the first phrase needs to be commented on. "No house-servant can serve two masters." The Greek for serve is *douleuein*. It comes from the basic noun *doulos*, which means a bond-slave. The verb *douleuein* is the present infinitive of *douleuoo*, "to work or work in bondage, to be subjugated." The tense indicates constant slave labor from which there can be no escape. This verb stands in contrast to *ergazomai* which merely means to labor (Matt. 21:28; 25:28) for the purpose of a set recompense. It is from the noun *ergon*, "work," from which this verb is derived and, as a noun, stands in antithesis to *charis*, "grace."

Our Lord is saying that we cannot be constantly, slavishly laboring for two masters or lords at one and the same time. We should slavishly work for our Lord considering Him master of all, and at the same time work (*ergazesthai*) for a set reward in order to live in this physical world of ours. This is equivalent to the Christian being in the world but not of the world (John 17:12, 14-17). As Christians, we are not to quit our work and get rid of all our possessions and relatives, but beware lest any of these become our God. They have their place and should be kept there.

Our Lord therefore was not referring to occasionally doing some work for mammon, but being enslaved to him and constantly laboring for him. If we do that, we cannot be His disciple as He clearly stated in Luke 14:26 and Matthew 10:37. Therefore, what He was actually saying in Luke 16:13 and Matthew 6:24 was: Allow me to see whose slavish laborer you are and I'll tell you who is your master. You cannot say you have Me as your Master and be slavishly laboring for this world having made whoever or whatever your god.

Let me hold lightly
Things of this earth;

Transient treasures,
  What are they worth?
Moths can corrupt them,
  Rust can decay;
All their bright beauty
  Fades in a day.
Let me hold lightly
  Temporal things—
I, who am deathless,
  I, who wear wings!

Let me hold fast, Lord,
  Things of the skies;
Quicken my vision,
  Open my eyes!
Show me Thy riches,
  Glory, and grace,
Boundless as time is,
  Endless as space . . . .

Let me hold lightly
  Things that were mine—
Lord, Thou dost give me
  All that is Thine!
                    Martha Snell Nicholson

There can really only be one of two masters. Christ, God
incarnate, or mammon, incarnate in people or things. If you
attempt to have both as masters, then this is what is going to
happen. You are going to hate the one or you are going to
love the other. That they are different is made clear from the
two Greek words used: "the one"—*ton hena,* and "the
other"—*ton heteron.* That Greek word *heteron* means
another of a different kind or quality. Using the word
"another" as a simple numerical quantity would have been
indicated by the word *allon.* The one deserves to be hated

and the other deserves to be loved. Now, the word "hate" as we explained in the context of Luke 14:26-33 and Matthew 10:37 means to "love less than the Lord." That's what the Lord implies here. He said it more explicitly in Luke 14:23, 33, and Matthew 7:37. If any relative or belonging is allowed by you to become your unrighteous mammon, then he or it ought to be hated. That hatred actually should be turned against your own self for allowing yourself to be brought to such an untenable position. You cannot make your parent or your spouse or your child or your possession your god and still claim that Jesus Christ occupies first place. It is impossible. Put each relative and possession away from you into their proper category (apotassomai—Luke 9:61; 14:33) and place God on the throne of your heart as Master. Only then will you know how to best manage your family and money. He who loves Christ most satisfies his family best and manages his earthly affairs most prudently. If you don't, then you are actually hating your relatives for your love to them is incongruent. You are giving to humans love which belongs to God. There is no shifting of love. Give God His due and then you will be able to give your family and possessions their proper and due attention.

He who is wise (sophos) toward God is prudent (phronimos) toward relatives, humans and possessions. After all, this is the theme of the parable: prudence, which is a balanced and proper relationship with our fellow humans and possessions. Peruse verse 8 of this parable again: "And the Lord commended the economist of unrighteousness (money) because he did or acted prudently. For the sons of this generation are more prudent than the sons of light in their own generation."

THINK IT OVER

1. What happens to one's love when another begins to take its place?

2. To whom do we owe our slavish allegiance? Why?
3. How can we best love our family? Why?

36

Harvest Time

The tenses of the verbs in the second clause of Luke 16:13 are worthy of note. "He will hate the one." The verb in Greek is *miseesei*, third person singular future indicative active of the verb *miseoo*, to hate. It has to happen if we elevate any person, no matter how close, or any possession to the place of a god. Remember what our Lord said in Luke 16:10-12. Anybody or anything of this earth is little or "least"; it is not absolutely dependable, because it is finite and ephemeral and does not become absolutely part of a person as God does. When, therefore, we make the little much while it is not, and the limited to be infinitely true, and embrace the strange as if it were ours, we can't help but reap a harvest of tears and disappointment. We will then hate it because it did not prove to be all that we thought it was going to be.

Sooner or later we are going to hate it, our Lord says, but He does not say when we are going to come to that realization. The time factor is not as important as the certainty of the realization that it will come sooner or later in this life or in the eternal habitations when we appear before the judgment seat of Christ.

"The other," (*heteron*-who is so different) "he will love." The tense of the verb "love" also is *agapeesei*, third person singular future of *agapoo*, "to love." This is going to take place at a particular time in the future. When? We are not told. The stress is on the certainty and not the time.

There is also a second contrast in the third clause of this verse: "or else he will hold to the one, and despise the other." Again, both of the verbs are in the future, emphasizing that we will eventually realize what we have done. The verb translated "will hold to " in Greek is *anthexetai*, third person singular future middle of *antechomai*, from *anti*, "against," and *echoo*, "to hold, adhere." It means to hold anything against a resisting force (here and in Titus 1:9 and I Thess. 5:14). The other verb translated "despise" is *kataphroneesi*, third person singular future indicative of *kataphroneoo*, from *kata*, "against or denoting ill feeling," and the verb *phroneoo*, "to think." It is to look down upon somebody, to think ill of him. Sooner or later, one object of affection is considered in contrast to the other, and then an abrasive action sets in. Very few things can resist disintegration under the perpetual motion of the grindstone. Recently, on our local television, a man was interviewed who supplied restaurants with knives for use in their kitchens. Daily, he would drop a freshly sharpened set of knives at each kitchen and pick up the used knives. I was amazed to hear that knives with blades as wide as two or three inches were reduced to uselessness due to the constant grinding and sharpening in a matter of less than a month.

Can we find the love of Christ sufficient and satisfying if we are with one hand trying to hold on to Him, but with the other feed our selfish appetites? The worldly appetite is a tapeworm within us. The more we feed it, the more it grows, and the hungrier we become. Our spiritual lives become emaciated and sickly, and by and by, the lust of the world wins out and the buoyant glow of the dedicated Christian wanes. The abrasive action of the world has won.

If you try this impossible experiment, Christ says, to have two equal masters simultaneously in your life, some time in the future you are going to be attached to the one and you are going to despise the other.

You cannot love two wives equally simultaneously. Why? Because each one deserves a special place and the same spot in your life. There can be only one filling that spot. But you can love both a father and a mother, an aunt and an uncle, two children and so on. Why? Because there is a spot in your heart and life for each one of them. But the throne of your heart is exclusively for one who is above and beyond you— God. And you dare not put anyone in the place of God as you dare not put any other woman or man in the place of your spouse. If you do, only one thing can happen. You will draw closer to the one and will drop the other. It cannot be otherwise.

The second and third clauses of this verse are actually suppositional. The Lord said it is impossible for a servant or for anyone to have two masters. Why?

Let us just suppose it were possible. What would happen?

At some time in the future, such a person will hate the one and will love the other. He will be attached to the one and despise the other. Therefore it is impossible to have two masters or two wives occupying the same allegiance because there is room only for one. Why try it since the results are certain? I tell you so, affirms Christ. These are laws written indelibly in the nature of things. I know since I have created them. Sooner or later you are going to realize this. Therefore don't allow appearances to pass as realities, and don't allow things strange to you to appear as becoming part of you for they can never really be.

Hating Means to Properly Evaluate and Love

The Lord said these words to cause His disciples to give due respect and recognition to relatives, friends, humans, possessions and situations in life. He never asked His disciples to hate either their fellow humans or their possessions. How could He, having told them that they should love even their enemies (Matt. 5:44)? He simply intimated that their love for these could not be equated with the love and devotion due to Himself. If they did, the love for the one would suffer. But no one would suffer more than the one trying the experiment, because God would not mean to him all that He wants to mean to him or be able to be to him all that He wants to be. And what he has chosen to accomplish for God's work in his life, he will never be able to do.

In II Kings 17:24-41, we have a very fine illustration of what man is always tempted to try. The Assyrians who were not worshipers of the true God conquered a certain area. After the Assyrians settled there, some lions came and destroyed their property. They presumed that this evil happened to them because their people did not worship the God of that particular land. What did they do? They found a priest who instructed them in the religion of Israel. However, they did not forsake their idols. They tried to follow what the priest taught them about the worship of the God of the Israelites but at the same time continued to hold to their idols. It is said about them: "So these nations feared the Lord, and served their graven images" (II Kings 17:41). It was the idols who were really their God, for they never forsook them to become totally attached to the God of Israel.

These are those who are of the world and are in the church. They are not believers. In reality, they labor for mammon. These are the ones who were justifying themselves before men, the hypocrites who never belonged to Christ. The more of the world and their own righteousness they had, the more they hated Christ.

There are those, however, who are Christ's, who have made a commitment to Him for salvation, but who have a hard time letting go of people and property. As long as we live in the world, the attempt of mammon and all that he represents will be to dethrone God. Those efforts of the evil one will fail, but nevertheless, they deprive us of the joy of full surrender.

No one really knows the compromises Christians make in this life at the detriment of their Lord and His kingdom. I don't believe the measurement of our commitment to Him with what it could have been will be fully revealed and realized by us until the day of the *beema*, the judgment of Christ.

That is what Paul in Romans 8:19 calls the manifestation of the sons of God. In translating this important verse literally from the Greek, this is what we have: "For the earnest expectation of the creation (the entire universe) waiteth eagerly for the revelation of the sons of God." The term for "sons" here is *huioi*, referring to growth in our spiritual lives. At the second coming, when we shall all appear before the beema judgment, we'll know how much of the joy of the Lord we missed for having loved this world even as Demas did who forsook Paul when he needed him most in his imprisonment in Rome (II Tim. 4:10).

This is exactly what Paul also says to the Corinthians who were believers but constantly flirting with the world. "Every man's work shall be made manifest: for the day shall declare it, because it shall be revealed by fire; and the fire shall try every man's work of what sort it is. If any man's work abide which he hath built thereupon, he shall receive a reward. If any man's work shall be burned, he shall suffer loss: but he himself shall be saved; yet as by fire" (I Cor. 3:13-15).

Punishments in heaven are the loss of the possible reward. A child minds more the privation of a reward as punishment rather than corporeal punishment. Such will be our heavenly loss for any compromises with the world. How would we feel if, when we get to heaven, we will find other Christians being welcomed there by many who were won by earthly mammon of unrighteousness, money, which they made their servant instead of their master. We may hardly have any to welcome us there. Our welcoming committee in heaven will be proportionate to our sacrifice for Christ on earth. The choice how we manage our money is ours. But the consequences of that choice are fixed.

Few of us have ever heard of John Livingstone, the brother of the famous missionary, David Livingstone. When John Livingstone died, he was one of the wealthiest men in his country. The two boys grew up together in Scotland in the same home and received the same instruction. In time, each made a choice for his own life. John determined to acquire wealth rather than follow Christ. David obeyed the command of Christ: "If any man will come after me, let him deny himself, and take up his cross, and follow me" (Matt. 16:24). John lived in luxury and wealth. David died in a miserable hut in Africa. When John died, however, there was only a brief note in the obituary column telling of his passing and of his being a brother of David Livingstone. But can you imagine the multitude of souls who constituted David Livingstone's welcoming committee in heaven?

Think of your welcoming committee. How big is it going to be? Know this for sure: in heaven will be revealed the final result of everything you did and gave during your earthly walk of faith. Every dime you gave, every word you uttered in witness or intercessory prayer, everything you have written, every telephone call and visit you made—you'll know what souls were influenced for Christ. Don't for one moment think that God does not maintain a memory bank. If man can build computers with memory, just imagine what God can do! There is coming "the revelation of the sons of God" when all works of faith will be fully manifested. No wonder Paul says that "the whole creation is on its tiptoes, with head protruding, looking forward to it." That is actually what Romans 8:19 speaks about as one analyzes it in the Greek text.

A preacher was traveling in a train. Sitting behind him was an elderly lady with four poorly dressed children. One of them began to repeatedly bump against the back of the gentleman.

The preacher's first impulse was speak roughly to the boy and reprimand him. Instead, he spoke kindly to the child and bought candy for him and the other children. Then he told them Bible stories.

Several hours passed. As the train neared the preacher's destination, a well-dressed gentleman approached him and said, "The other passengers and I have observed with admiration your kindness to these children. That's real Christianity!"

"I don't understand," said the preacher.

"You did not know it," the gentleman replied, "but the elderly lady with these children is not their mother. Their mother is in the baggage car in her casket."

Can you imagine how that mother would welcome the preacher in heaven with such gratitude for what he had done for her children!

Don't ever think that what you do for Christ on earth, no

229

matter how small, will not have its heavenly reward!

You cannot serve two masters, God and mammon. Why not now become a prudent manager of your money?

THINK IT OVER

1. What happens when we try to serve two masters?
2. What did Christ mean when He told us to hate the things of the world?
3. What did Paul mean by "the manifestation of the sons of God" in Romans 8:19?
4. What are punishments in heaven?
5. How can we assure ourselves of a large welcoming committee in heaven?

I

INDEX OF SUBJECTS

Subject   *Page*

(For fuller index see Index of Greek Words)

II

INDEX OF ENGLISH WORDS

233

III

INDEX OF GREEK WORDS

239

prassoo,			
prattoo	do	Luke 22:33;	
		23:15	88
praxis	deed, act	Matt. 16:27	
		Luke 23:51	
		Acts 19:18	88
psychee	soul, life		170, 202
ptoochos,			
penees	poor	Luke 16:20	117
skeenee	habitation,	Luke 16:9	
	tabernacle, tent	Matt. 17:4	
		II Peter 1:13,	50, 54
		14	67
sophos	wise	Matt. 11:25;	
		23:34	
		Luke 10:21	70, 75
		Rom. 1:14	78, 221
storgee			
(astorgoi)	family love	II Tim. 3:3	178
sunetos	right judgements,		
	wrong behavior		76
tassoo	categorize, set in	Luke 7:8	
	place	Acts 15:2;	
		22:10; 28:23;	
		Rom. 13:1	
		I Cor. 16:15	169
topos	place	John 14:2	61, 62
zeeteoo	seek		203

IV

INDEX OF SCRIPTURE VERSES

V

ILLUSTRATION INDEX

NOTES

NOTES

NOTES

NOTES

NOTES

NOTES

NOTES

Other Books by Dr. Spiros Zodhiates

Studies on Luke

Studies in John's Gospel

Studies on James

Three-Volume Set in handsome slip cover

Miscellaneous Titles

Spiros Zodhiates was born on the island of Cyprus, of Greek parents. After completing his Greek education, he attended the American University in Cairo, Egypt, and New York University in the United States. He holds the degrees of Th.B., M.A. and Th.D. In 1946 he came to the United States at the invitation of American Mission to Greeks, Inc., of which he is now President. Founded in 1942, it was a one-room, two-part-time-employee organization when Spiros Zodhiates undertook its leadership. Now, as AMG International, it occupies its own international headquarters building at 6815 Shallowford Road, Chattanooga, Tennessee, and carries on a world-wide evangelistic and relief ministry.

The author is a recognized authority on the Greek New Testament, and edited an edition of the Modern Greek New Testament published by the Million Testaments Campaigns and the American Bible Society. He is the author of numerous exegetical Bible-study books and booklets in both Greek and English.

Spiros Zodhiates speaks daily and Sunday on the New Testament Light radio program, released over a special network of stations across the United States and in Canada. This is an English-language program, primarily concerned with expounding the Greek New Testament. He is responsible for introducing the Modern Greek pronunciation of Classical and Koine Greek into U.S. colleges and universities, through a Guide to Modern Greek Pronunciation and his tape recordings of the entire Koine New Testament (Nestle's Text) in Modern pronunciation. These recordings are available on cassettes. They may be ordered from AMG Publishers, Chattanooga, Tennessee 37422.